Date Due

ZURAug92		
DEC 12 1995		
DEC 16 '95		

BRODART, INC. Cat. No. 23 233 Printed in U.S.A.

8024

Reid, Scott, 1964-
  Canada remapped : how the partition of Quebec will reshape the nation / Scott Reid. -- Vancouver : Pulp Press, c1992.
  xi, 184 p. : ill.

Includes bibliographical references (p. 174-178) and index.
06375103 ISBN:0889782490 (pbk.)

DISCARD

1. Quebec (Province) - History - Autonomy and independence movements. 2. Quebec (Province) -
(SEE NEXT CARD)

CANADA REMAPPED

*How the Partition of Quebec
Will Reshape the Nation*

SCOTT REID

**PULP
PRESS**

VANCOUVER

*To the wise and tolerant electors of Berne and the Jura,
in the hope that Canadians will have the generosity
and foresight to follow their example.*

CANADA REMAPPED
Copyright © 1992 Scott Reid

PULP PRESS
Arsenal Pulp Press Ltd.
100-1062 Homer Street
Vancouver, B.C.
Canada V6B 2W9

The publisher gratefully acknowledges the ongoing assistance of
The Canada Council and The Cultural Services Branch, B.C. Min-
istry of Tourism and Minister Responsible for Culture.

Typeset by the Vancouver Desktop Publishing Centre
Printed by Webcom
Printed and bound in Canada

CANADIAN CATALOGUING IN PUBLICATION DATA:
Reid, Scott, 1964-
  Canada remapped

  Includes bibliographical references and index.
  ISBN 0-88978-249-0

  1. Quebec (Province)—History—Autonomy and independence
movements. 2. Quebec (Province)—Politics and government—
1985- * I. Title.
FC2925.9.S4R44 1992   971.4′04   C92-091179-X
F1053.2.R44 1992

CONTENTS

ACKNOWLEDGEMENTS

I am grateful to a number of people, without whom this book would not have been possible: Larry Thompson, my editorial assistant, whose guidance and intuition helped me mould this book; Stephanie Mullen, who worked with remarkable efficiency as my research assistant; Brian Lam at Pulp Press; David Thorpe for his help in preparing the maps; Stefan Paquette for explaining some of the finer points in Bernese constitutional law; Suzanne Fraser for editorial work and proofreading; Laurie Heffernan for fast and efficient typing; the staff at the Directeur-général des élections in Quebec City, who were most patient with my endless requests for poll maps and statistical data; K.D. McRae of Carleton University; my father, Gordon Reid, for stressing at all points during the development of this book that even in separation the aspirations of English Canada cannot be met if those of French Canada are not fairly respected; Lionel Albert, who was kind enough to help me with a very early draft of this work; and Bill and Kathy Bradford and Timothy Virkkala at Liberty Publishing in Washington, for their help and encouragement at the very beginning.

Finally, I must reserve special thanks to my wonderful wife, Poh Lan, for her patience, perseverance, and long-standing faith in me. I hope her love and loyalty may yet find its just reward.

Foreword
by Peter Brimelow

This remarkable book and its author, Scott Reid, are evidence that the political culture of English Canada can never be written off . . . completely. Just because English Canadian politicians appear to be certifiably brain-dead, and its intellectuals and publicists co-opted, corrupt, or cowed, does not mean that nothing is going on out there in the depths.

It is because there is something going on out there in the depths that English and French Canada will eventually succeed in resolving their co-habitation quandary, peacefully and honourably, despite the best efforts of a political class selfishly convinced its own interests require that both the English- and French-speaking nations in Canada be kept harnessed together in tandem.

For almost twenty years, I have been pontificating about Canada in the pages of the *Financial Post*, the Toronto *Sun* and its sister papers, and (improbable as it may sound) *Maclean's* magazine. Journalism in Canada is like life in a small town, and you soon become aware of powerful social taboos. In 1969, when Peter Desbarats collaborated with René Lévesque in an interview imagining an independent Quebec, English Canadian newspapers refused to carry the result on the grounds that it made separation appear too credible. In 1976, I caused a very uncomfortable silence in a *Maclean's* editorial meeting by commenting that our projections for the imminent Quebec provincial election implied the PQ would, for the first time, win a majority of francophone votes. Actually, of course, Lévesque and the Parti Québécois won outright and we had to tear the magazine apart. In 1982—just to show how far these taboos extend—the academic editors of the Atlantic Council's authoritative survey, *Canada and the United States: Dependence and Divergence,* felt obliged to append a note to a perfectly sensible essay on Quebec recording that members of their working group had objected, not merely to the author's mildly pro-nationalist conclusions, but to any essay on Quebec *at all.*

By contrast, Canadian readers seem models of cool common sense. The mail that came into *Maclean's* in 1976, for example, made it plain that many Canadians were distinctly more willing to contemplate the possible departure of Quebec than was their "National Newsmagazine." Over the years, I have been privileged—and it is a privilege—to receive a lot of this dissident correspondence. But I have rarely been more impressed than when I opened the envelope that contained an early draft of this book.

Scott Reid combines great erudition, analytical power, political judgement, gifts of exposition, and—rarest of all—imagination. He makes a case for an amicable negotiated partition of Quebec that cannot be ignored. This is a formidable achievement for a writer still in his twenties, working entirely independently of Canada's media and academic establishment. Canada must hope and expect to hear from him again.

In my own book on Canada, *The Patriot Game: Canada and the Canadian Question Revisited,* I concluded that getting Quebec out of Confederation would be a good thing for English Canada regardless of its effects on Quebec—indeed, that the issue might ultimately be not whether Quebec would secede, but whether it should be expelled (which is what the Malaysians did with Singapore.) Because of that, and because I see no point in permanently alienating Quebec, I have always tended to downplay the possibility of partition. It seemed to me to be an entirely reasonable goal for Anglo-Quebecers, but not central to the interests of the rest of English Canada.

I still think that Quebec will probably leave Confederation in one piece. But Scott Reid has convinced me that the sort of minimalist partition he suggests would be a desirable refinement.

It is worth stressing two further points. Firstly, most earlier partition plans—proposed, needless to say, by other enterprising non-establishment individuals—have been designed to intimidate Quebec from seceding, or to punish it if it did. But under this plan, Quebec would give up only about one-half of one percent of its territory (provided it can convince its aboriginal population that its generous rhetoric about Native self-government is sincere). The new state would eliminate more than half of its million or so non-francophones and end its minority problem. At the same time, it could gain francophone areas from the rest of Canada. Although Scott Reid expresses the hope that his plan will help maintain Canadian unity, it seems to me that his partition plan could actually facilitate Quebec's move to sovereignty.

Secondly, the spirit that informs this work is that of liberty. It is in an environment of free trade and free movement that the civilized system of enclaves and exclaves that has accommodated Switzerland's ethnic divisions can work best. It is where governments are intrusive and centralized that conflict is most easily generated. Unfortunately, the latter pretty well describes the imperial state now administered by the mandarinate in Ottawa.

As this book goes to press, we do not know if the National Unity Industry will succeed in staving off this latest Quebec crisis. But we can be sure the crisis will recur, again and again, until there is an institutional solution to the problem of two nations in one state.

If the history of the Canada-U.S. Free Trade Agreement is any guide, Canadians will wake up one morning to find that their politicians, struggling for a momentary advantage, have suddenly adopted some scheme previously denounced as unworkable, unthinkable, etc. All sides will be lucky if the scheme is that so ably elaborated here by Scott Reid.

Peter Brimelow is the author of The Patriot Game: Canada and the Canadian Question Revisited *and Senior Editor at* Forbes Magazine *in New York.*

Introduction

Imagining the Unimaginable

Imagine a country of soaring mountains, vast forests, and dramatic seacoasts. Imagine that this country has approximately 25 million citizens, not all of whom speak the same language or share the same culture. This country is a union of nations.

One of these nations, with a population of about five million, prides itself on its distinctness and considers itself to have the right of self-determination. For years attempts are made to accommodate the needs of this nation. The federation becomes decentralized, adopting unconventional constitutional arrangements which are hopelessly impractical. Even the country's leading institutions are rearranged on ethnic lines. But ultimately there is no satisfying the minority nationality, and the federal government refuses to make further concessions. A referendum is held in the minority nation and more than half the population votes for separation. Independence is declared.

There is a problem. Within the boundaries of the newly independent nation there are enclaves of territory inhabited by people of the majority nationality. Fearing discrimination, this minority-within-a-minority demands federal protection. The enclaves hold their own referenda, then declare themselves to have separated from the newly independent republic. But the new republic does not recognize their right of secession. Federal troops intervene to protect the enclaves. Skirmishes with the republican militia are reported. Civil war follows.

The 'anonymous' federation described above is Yugoslavia. The minority nation is Croatia, and the minority-within-a-minority are the 500,000 Serbs who live within Croatia's borders. The scenario could equally describe Canada in 1993, if we make enough of the same mistakes as the Yugoslavs made.

The parallels between Canada and Yugoslavia are surprisingly extensive. Both have populations of roughly 25 million. Both federations contain an independent-minded minority nation of about 5 million. Just as Croatia is home to half a million Serbs who want out, Quebec contains over one million non-francophones. This minority wants no part of an independent republic.

Canada and Quebec: The Inevitable Crisis

If Quebec separates from Canada an attempt will be made to partition the new country. This is not a threat; it is a simple fact. As long ago as 1978, Marie-Josée Drouin and Brian Bruce-Biggs of the Hudson Institute warned:

> If Quebec goes out, and any significant portion of the province wants to stay in Canada and demands the protection of the Canadian government, that government [will have] very little choice but to go along. Irredentism would inevitably flourish in the rump of Quebec.[1]

More recently, a senior Bell Canada executive addressing a symposium hosted by the prestigous C.D. Howe Institute expressed the fear that "the possibility of revoking provincial boundaries ... would provoke the worst irredentist nightmares that I could imagine."[2]

Even Brian Mulroney is aware of the dangers. Although he carefully avoided any direct reference to partition, the Prime Minister observed in a recent interview that:

> ... nobody should make any smug assumptions—that you can chop off a part of the country and the rest of the country is going to continue to function in a neat, tidy, effective way, because it may not. No one should assume anymore that the Yugoslavs or the Soviets or anybody else [are exceptions], that there's something in the air we breathe that makes us immune

from certain realities. Or that once the process begins, that it is going to be affectionate and tidy and warm and civilized.[3]

Today, partition is the official policy of two political parties in Quebec. The Equality Party favours partition in the event of separation. They currently hold four seats in the Quebec National Assembly. At the federal level, the Option Canada Party favours partition and the creation of an eleventh province even if Quebec does not secede. They plan to run candidates in the next federal election.

Poll evidence suggests that the partition question will polarize and radicalize public opinion in Quebec like no other issue. An Angus Reid poll conducted in late April and early May 1991 indicates that 12 percent of Quebecers favour partition in the event of separation, while 82 percent are opposed to it. Although an ethnic breakdown of the responses was not given, these percentages correspond almost exactly with Quebec's ethnic breakdown: 12 percent anglophone, 84 percent francophone. An unusually small number of those polled (6 percent) were undecided. This is a sign of an emotional, polarized debate. In the other provinces, where the partition issue was not yet well known, the undecided factor was 50 percent higher.[4]

The figures suggest that when it comes fully into public focus in the rest of Canada, the partition issue will divide Canadians neatly along ethno-linguistic lines, with francophones unanimously opposing it and all non-francophone groups favouring the idea.

The ability of this issue to cause polarization and acrimony should not be underestimated. Poll data from another partition, which took place in Switzerland about fifteen years ago, show that a large body of moderate opinion can exist as long, and only as long, as compromise is a realistic option. In Canada the moderate group would be the supporters of an unpartitioned Quebec in an undivided Canada.

Once some dramatic event like a majority 'Yes' vote in a referendum on independence makes it clear that unity must be shattered, it is no longer possible to divide one's loyalty between the province and the country. By necessity, even moderates are forced to choose sides. Those who offer their loyalty to the emerging polity demand that its existing territorial boundaries be respected, while those who remain loyal to the old country cry out for a partition that will let them be citizens of the country of their own choosing.

Ethnic Polarization in Switzerland

Figures from the Swiss example show just how extreme the polar-ization can become. When the French-speaking Jura region sepa-rated from the German-majority canton of Berne in the 1970s, several rounds of voting were held. The first round was similar to the Quebec referendum of 1980, in that all voters were asked to choose whether or not they wished to see the Jura region secede. In subsequent rounds of voting, individual communes (townships) were given the option of seceding from the soon-to-be-separate Jura in order to rejoin Berne.

In the first round, the percentage difference in votes between the communes that would eventually choose to remain in Berne and those that would choose to join the Jura was 50 percent, roughly the same level of polarization as existed in Quebec at the time of the 1980 referendum (when about half of francophones voted 'Yes' and virtually all minorities voted 'No'). By the time the Jurassians had completed the third round of voting, ethnic differences had har-dened and the gap had grown to 77 percent.[5]

Ethnic Polarization in Yugoslavia

A plebiscite was held on May 12, 1991, in the Serbian-majority Krajina region in the Republic of Croatia. It presented the following question: if Croatia separated from Yugoslavia , did the electorate wish Krajina to become part of Serbia? Seventy-three percent of eligible voters turned out to cast their ballots and a full 99 percent of participants voted 'Yes.' It appears that virtually every Serbian voter participated, while almost every Croat in the region boy-cotted the vote. In a Croatia-wide referendum held a few days later, the vast majority of ethnic Croats voted to secede from Yugoslavia. The Serbian minority refused to participate in this vote. Within two months, Serbia and Croatia were at war.

In Croatia, partition has led to civil war, while in the Jura the issue was resolved peacefully. Yet in both cases, an attempt had been made at democracy and the use of local referenda. In the case of Yugoslavia it was notably unsuccessful. In the first two chapters of this book I will explore the reasons for this apparent contradic-tion.

In the remainder of the book, I will show how Canada can emulate the Swiss example and avoid repeating the Yugoslav experience. The method I will recommend for accomplishing this goal is to follow the example of the Jura partition as closely as possible, adapting it where necessary to the somewhat different circumstances of the Quebec context.

Guns and Mutterers

The Front de Libération du Québec (FLQ) bombings and kidnappings of 1963-1970 revealed to a startled Canadian nation that even this country has the potential for violence. The entire October Crisis was caused by a mere handful of individuals armed with a few guns and possessing a rudimentary knowledge of bomb construction. There was no dramatic, sudden crisis that inspired Paul Rose and his comrades to launch their campaign of violence. The FLQ surfaced out of the general sense of dissatisfaction that had caused the Quiet Revolution in Quebec. Today's talk of partition, and tomorrow's potential territorial disputes, have the potential to be a far greater incitement to action than anything that motivated the murderers of Pierre Laporte.

What is the potential for violence? Some of the partition proposals coming from English Canadian advocates of partition are considerably more extreme than anything the Serbs have ever proposed for Croatia. Before civil war broke out in Yugoslavia, the Serbs were demanding only the return of lands occupied by their countrymen. Some English Canadians favour seizing four-fifths of Quebec's landmass—territory containing over half of the province's francophone population, and Quebec government assets totalling billions of dollars. If Serbia's demands led to civil war, what on earth are the noises emanating from English Canada likely to cause if they are ever taken seriously? Perhaps some Canadians think we will be able to avoid violence simply because our countrymen are more civilized than the Serbs and Croats, but I wouldn't want to build an entire partition plan based solely on this assumption.

We Need a Plan

What Canada needs to do instead is to develop a federal law governing the mechanics both of separation and of partition. This law must be realistic and practical, because we may have to implement it. Some readers may object to this on the grounds that it would give official sanction to the concept of separation. This is true, but the objection comes a bit late. After all, what greater sanction could be given to Quebec's right of self-determination than the active participation of the prime minister and federal cabinet in the 1980 referendum? On the other hand, the law would give Canada, for the first time, a realistic chance to ensure that partition would peacefully and justly take place.

A partition law would also demonstrate that independence carries a price-tag. Canada's leaders have recognized Quebec's right to separate, but they refuse to attach costs to it, for fear of alienating the Quebec vote. This may make good partisan sense, but it also plays into the hands of Quebec's separatist leaders. It is the surest way of guaranteeing a 'Yes' vote in the 1992 referendum on independence.

If it fails to adopt a partition law in advance, Canada may well be forced to produce a list of non-negotiable terms and conditions *after* a majority 'Yes' vote in the referendum. This would at best be perceived in Quebec as desperate and unbecoming behaviour. More likely, it would be seen as a vindictive, war-like power-play, and a good reason to unilaterally declare independence at once, whatever the cost, in order to pre-empt partition.

Following this, Canada could either shrug off the loss and let Quebec secede intact, or it could try to regain the parts it wants by force of arms. In this second scenario, Canada is already acting like Serbia.

If Canadians feel, as I believe they do, that the methods employed by both Serbia and Croatia are uncivilized, then they must talk *now* about the partition of Quebec in terms of civility, rather than in terms of greed, vindictiveness, and violence. What follows is a suggestion for a civilized solution to a Canadian national crisis.

CHAPTER ONE

Pride, Prejudice, and Partition in Northern Ireland and Yugoslavia

Canada is not the first country to be faced with the challenge of partitioning a seceding province or territory. We can learn much from the difficult experiences of some of the other countries that have tried their hands at the process. This chapter will review the unsuccessful British partition of Ireland in 1921, and the recent Serbian attempt to redefine Croatia's boundaries so as to exclude that republic's Serbian minority. Both of these partitions led to civil conflict, and each one provides lessons about how not to carry out a partition.

THE IRISH PARTITION OF 1921

The Irish Context

Irish nationalism was a growing problem for Great Britain throughout the nineteenth and early twentieth centuries, although the history of Irish restiveness dates back to the first English invasion in 1175. In the final century of its rule over Ireland, Britain faced perpetual rebelliousness in the Irish provinces, as well as the acute embarrassment of knowing that British rule in Ireland had historically been as unjust as anything perpetuated overseas by Britain's less civilized imperial rivals. By the second decade of the twentieth century, it was clear that Ireland would have to be granted some form of self-government.

Home rule was finally guaranteed in 1914 by the *Government of Ireland Act*. However, Northern Ireland's 820,000 Protestants

considered themselves to be loyal British subjects. Fearing that
their rights would not be respected in a Catholic-dominated Irish
state, they requested a partition based on religious affiliation. The
British government began to explore possible formulae for partitioning Ireland along religious lines, including plans for a parish-
by-parish division.

The outbreak of the First World War brought an end to these
plans. Home rule was put on hold until the end of hostilities. In
1916 a rebellion was launched in Dublin. It was quickly suppressed, but the execution of fifteen of its leaders won enormous
sympathy in Ireland for the nationalist cause. The rebel cause was
further helped by the introduction early in 1918 of a military service
bill that would have extended wartime conscription to Ireland.
Although the bill was never implemented, it was used as a rallying
point by the separatist party, Sinn Fein, in the general election of
1918. In this election seventy-three of the 106 Irish seats were taken
by Sinn Feiners, who then met in Dublin and declared themselves
to be Ireland's National Assembly, or *Dáil*.

The Dáil lacked the strength to enforce its claim to sovereignty,
and it could not openly support the terrorist campaign that followed between 1918 and 1921. Radicals took to shooting policemen
in the streets and attacking police stations. Supplementary troops
(called 'Black-and-Tans' for the colour of their uniforms) were
brought in from England to control the situation. However, their
presence made things worse. The counter-terrorist measures used
by the Black-and-Tans led to a rapid escalation of the conflict. Soon
the terrorists were striking at anyone who dared to express a
pro-British opinion, while the Black-and-Tans at one point burned
down part of the city of Cork as a retaliatory measure.

Britain's moral authority to rule Ireland had been based upon its
respect for the law. This eroded as it adopted the tactics of the
terrorists. By 1921, many Englishmen, including the Archbishop of
Canterbury, had publicly condemned the British actions. The government was forced to pass a new home rule law dividing Ireland into
two sections. The nationalists and the British then signed a treaty
recognizing the supremacy of the Dáil in Southern Ireland.

The Anglo-Irish Treaty of 1921 and the Irish Boundary
Commission of 1925

The Anglo-Irish Treaty of 1921 awarded Southern Ireland (known as the Irish Free State) twenty-six of Ireland's thirty-two counties, while the British-ruled North was awarded the remaining six. This division was intended to ensure that as few Protestants as possible would be left in the Catholic-dominated Free State.

The partition was regarded as being arbitrary even by its British authors, and was intended to be a purely temporary arrangement, until the borders could be redrawn. It had the effect of leaving 430,000 Catholics in Northern Ireland, where they formed about 34 percent of the population.[6]

At first the British tried to act with magnanimity and good sense towards the Nationalists in the Irish Free State on the one hand, and the Unionists in the North on the other. One symptom of a growing intransigence on all sides was the failure of a multilateral boundary commission in the mid-1920s to come up with substantive changes to the frontier. The proposed changes were so insignificant that they were rejected by the Free State as worse than the status quo. In the end the Nationalists vented their anger over the unfair border by adopting an amendment to the Free State's constitution, laying claim to all of the North. British troops ensured that Northern Ireland's boundaries would remain for the next three-quarters of a century exactly as they had been demarcated in 1921. Decades of terrorism and irredentism have been the result.

Why The Irish Boundary Commission Failed

Under the terms of Article XII of the Anglo-Irish Treaty of 1921, a three-man boundary commission was appointed to determine a new boundary which was more fair than the one that had been awarded in the 1921 partition. The first commissioner was to represent the Irish Free State, while the second represented Northern Ireland. The chairman, Justice Richard Feetham of the South African Supreme Court, represented the British government. Feetham was the British government's second choice after the former Canadian prime minister, Sir Robert Borden, who turned down the post.

The Commission met for the first time on November 6, 1924. It had been delayed for over a year by the refusal of the Northern Ireland government to appoint a commissioner. Throughout the life of the Commission, the government of Northern Ireland did what it could to disrupt its proceedings. There was general satisfaction with the existing border among the Unionists who dominated the government of Ulster, because it kept almost all of Ireland's Protestant population on British soil.

The Commission's work continued until November 1925, when its recommended changes were leaked to the press—possibly by the commissioner from Northern Ireland. The commissioner from the Irish Free State resigned shortly afterwards as public pressures mounted in the Free State against any surrender of territory to the North. (A few small transfers of Protestant-dominated pockets owned by the Free State had been included in the proposals.)

When it became clear that the Commission's proposals had no chance of being put into effect, the Boundary Commission's report was suppressed on the initiative of the Irish and British prime ministers. It was locked away from public view for over forty years.

Two of the three commissioners, Feetham and Eóin MacNeill of the Free State, had been sincere in their desire to find a satisfactory solution to the boundary problem, and they seem to have predominated over their colleague from Northern Ireland. Yet their enterprise was doomed from the start by the circumstances of the political environment in which they were required to work and by the restrictions placed on their mandate.

The Commission's task had been to find a more equitable and just solution to the boundary question than the one that had been imposed in 1921. In doing so, it was instructed to "determine in accordance with the wishes of the inhabitants, so far as may be compatible with economic and geographic conditions, the boundary between Northern Ireland and the rest of Ireland."[7]

The mandate was full of ambiguities. For example, the word "inhabitants" implies areas of inhabitation. These areas were not defined. Was the boundary to be adjusted on the basis of majority wishes by municipality, by parish, or by some other unit of measure? The commissioners were forced to give an arbitrary definition to the meaning of "inhabitants."

Equally unclear was the extent to which majority rule was to be used as a guide to the wishes of the "inhabitants." Judge Feetham expressed his own confusion on the matter when he stated,

> If the Commission were to make a change in the boundary involving the transfer of an area containing 1,999 inhabitants simply in order to gratify 1,000 of such inhabitants at the cost of offending the other 999, such a proceeding would obviously be unreasonable. It would likewise be unreasonable if the

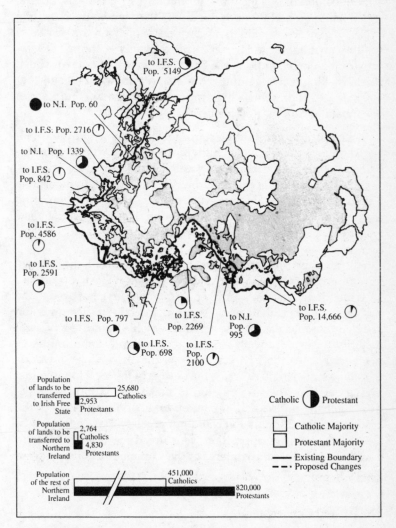

Recommendations of the Irish Boundary Commission of 1925. (Fig. 1)

> Commission were to decline to make a change involving the
> transfer of an area containing, say, 1,000 inhabitants, of whom
> all save two or three desired the change merely because of the
> opposition of this insignificant minority . . . . There is, I think,
> much to be said for adopting a rule that, where the case for a
> change of the existing boundary rests solely on the wishes of
> the inhabitants, and is not fortified by any economic or geo-
> graphic considerations, the Commission would not be justified
> in making a change unless the majority in favour is substan-
> tial—i.e., represents a high proportion of the total number of
> inhabitants of the area concerned.[8]

Feetham observed that no hard and fast rule could be established as to the size of this "high proportion." It varied substantially as other political and economic factors came into account.
Also, in the absence of popular votes it was difficult to determine
the wishes of the inhabitants. The commissioners worked on the
assumption (probably correct) that all Catholics were Nationalists
and all Protestants were Unionists, but were hindered by their
reliance on the out-of-date data of the 1911 census.

Still another problem related to the question of the relative
importance of the "economic and geographical" factors that had
been mentioned in the Commission's mandate, as compared to the
wishes of the local inhabitants. After much debate, the Commission
decided that enclaves would be unacceptable regardless of local
majority wishes. As well, the existence in some communities of
major public works projects, such as the Belfast water works,
would be sufficient to overrule the desires of the local inhabitants.

The need for the Commission to make such arbitrary judge-
ments left the impression among observers on both sides of the
border that the Commission could not possibly make a fair or just
award. The forces of opposition were already well provided with
ammunition before the contents of the Commission's report were
leaked in November 1925.

The Absent Consensus

The commissioners would have been far more successful, even
within the mangled and contradictory terms of their mandate, if
their findings had had the force of law. Instead, the Commission
was compelled to search for a compromise solution that would be

satisfactory to both Northern Ireland and the Irish Free State, rather than a solution based solely on impartial considerations. The Free State took the position that the extreme unfairness of the original partition meant that it was Britain's turn to make unilateral concessions. The Free State's representatives also feared that a new partition agreement which left large Catholic pockets in British territory would be interpreted as a sign that they were satisfied with half-measures. For these reasons, the Attorney General of the Free State testified before the Commission that his government would surrender no territory to Britain. As a frustrated Chairman Feetham observed, this effectively meant that:

> The Free State Government urge that determination of the boundaries involves a reconsideration of the whole area of Northern Ireland, and that the Commission in such a reconsideration must not be influenced by the existing boundary, except for the purpose of restricting the limits of its enquiry to the northern side of it . . . .[9]

The Chairman's own view was that this contention was unjustified. He believed that the Commission's terms of reference authorized it to look at both sides of the border, but that the changes involved should be limited to the periphery of each state. As well, Feetham probably knew it would have been politically difficult to convince the Protestants of Northern Ireland to consent to a partition involving the loss of several thousand of their co-religionists to the Irish Free State without the return of at least some Protestant territory as compensation.

The Commission's recommendations were largely an attempt to reconcile the incompatible positions of the Nationalists and Unionists, rather than to find a just or logical solution to the problem. The Commission confined itself in the end to studying only a swathe of territory stretching about six miles wide on each side of the existing border.

The End of the Commission

The Commission favoured the transfer of fourteen parcels of territory, containing a total of 25,680 Catholics and 2,953 Protestants, to the Free State. In return, the Free State would have to consent to return to British sovereignty four smaller parcels with a total Protestant population of 4,830 and a Catholic population of 2,764.[10]

Nearly 95 percent of Northern Ireland's Catholics would not have been affected at all by the partition, had it actually taken place.

By transferring far more Catholic territory to the Irish Free State than they were asking the Free State to give up, the commissioners hoped to satisfy the Irish nationalists. The commissioners also hoped to satisfy the leadership of Northern Ireland by transferring a greater Protestant population to the north than it was abandoning to the south. As is usually the case with this sort of compromise measure, the Commission's recommendations satisfied neither side.

In the end it was the government of the Free State that killed the partition process by refusing to adopt the Commission's recommendations. On November 16, 1925—only a week after the report had been leaked—Prime Minister Cosgrave of the Irish Free State wrote to his country's commissioner, Eóin MacNeill, warning him that, "As far as I can learn, the movement against any portion of our territory being transferred is growing."[11] He urged MacNeill to resign. Four days later, his advice was followed, and the Irish Boundary Commission was, for all practical purposes, dead.

THE CROATIAN PARTITION OF 1991

The Yugoslav Context

The Serbian attempt to partition Croatia following that country's declaration of independence in June 1991 is the closest parallel to the Canadian situation available for us to study. It is also one of the most difficult examples to understand, due to the Byzantine ethnic politics of Yugoslavia and the whole Balkan region. It is not without reason that the collapse of large multi-ethnic states into warring petty nationalities is known as 'Balkanization.'[12]

Yugoslavia is, or was, a country of just under 25 million people. It contains twenty-four indigenous ethnic groups, eight of which are powerful enough to have their own republic or province within the federation. Founded in 1918 as the Kingdom of the Serbs, Croats and Slovenes, the country was Serbian-dominated from the start. The Serbian royal house ruled over the entire kingdom, and all major cabinet posts were reserved for Serbs. The Croatian separatist movement had its first flowering in the period of the Yugoslav monarchy. King Alexander was assassinated in 1934 by a Croatian separatist.

During the Second World War, Croatia aligned itself with the Nazi invaders, carving a small empire out of territory which today belongs to the republics of Serbia and Bosnia-Hertzegovina. The expanded borders of the Croatian state placed almost all of Yugoslavia's Croats under the rule of a Croatian national government for the first time in history. This arrangement also subjected a huge Serbian minority as well as many Muslims to a regime that was notable for its cruelty to non-Croats. The Nazis and Croats co-operated in the commission of many ethnically-based atrocities, including the ones in which former United Nations Secretary General Kurt Waldheim is alleged to have participated.

Gunpoint Partitioning

Following the war the Communist regime of Marshal Tito partitioned Croatia, removing many of the minority areas from the republic and leaving a substantial Croatian population within the boundaries of Bosnia-Hertzegovina. Now it was the Croatians' turn to suffer barbarous treatment. Most of the captured soldiers of the Croatian *Ustasa* army were summarily executed upon their capture by Tito's partisans. Few survived a death march from Austria to the Romanian frontier.

Tito believed that Yugoslav unity would improve if substantial ethnic minorities continued to live within the borders of each republic, since these minorities would look to the federal government for protection. Even after he had partitioned it, postwar Croatia's population remained 12 percent Serbian. The Republic of Bosnia-Hertzegovina was 18 percent Croat. Within Yugoslavia as a whole, the Serbs (who constituted about 36 percent of the total Yugoslav population at the time of the 1981 census) formed substantial minorities within the boundaries of four of the country's republics and provinces.

The Dissolution of Yugoslavian Federalism

Tito's unity plans worked fairly well while he was alive. Following his death in 1980, the system of maintaining unity through the existence of ethnic minorities in each republic began to backfire.

In 1989, the Yugoslav federal government removed the autonomous status of the province of Kosovo, where a separatist

Yugoslavia's Ethnic Division. (Fig. 2)

movement had been gaining popularity. Kosovo, which was the heart of the medieval kingdom of Serbia, is populated by Albanians, but it has a substantial Serbian minority.

The Albanians rebelled when faced with the removal of autonomous status. By the beginning of 1990 the federal army had moved in and effectively placed Kosovo under Serbian military rule.

In early 1991, Serbian nationalists in the capital made it clear that they would not allow Stipe Mesic, a Croatian, to take his turn at the federal presidency, which rotates annually among Yugoslavia's major ethnic groups. It had become obvious that the federal government had nearly ceased to function.

Croatians feared that their republic would soon face the same treatment as Kosovo. They felt that independence, or at least a much more decentralized federal structure, was required to prevent a crackdown. When it became clear that a compromise solution would not be forthcoming, a referendum held on May 19, 1991 resulted in a 94 percent majority of the Croatian electorate voting in favour of independence. Meanwhile, the Serbs of the Krajina region in Croatia's southwest had held an unofficial referendum of their own on May 12. By a majority of 99 percent, the voters of Krajina favoured uniting with Serbia in the event of Croatian independence.

Compared with the tactics employed in Kosovo, an unofficial referendum on partition seems a civilized and democratic measure. Its failure to prevent the outbreak of civil war in Croatia holds an important lesson for the minorities of Quebec, particularly since the idea of holding unofficial referenda on partition is being considered by the Cree and other Quebec minorities.

Ethnic Stand-Offs: "We're Prepared To Fight . . . ."

The referendum process failed to lead to a peaceful partition because neither of the ethnic groups were willing to accept the legitimacy of the other side's right of secession. The reason for the overwhelming majority in the Krajina referendum was because only Serbs voted. Croats in the Krajina region regarded the exercise as an illegal farce, and boycotted it. No impartial observers from outside the region were on hand to monitor the results. This meant that no matter how carefully and fairly the results were tabulated, they could be construed by opponents of the vote as being rigged. The May 19 republic-wide vote was likewise invalidated by the refusal of the Serbian minority to participate. The extremely high majority in favour of separation (94 percent) was partly the result of this boycott. No balloting at all took place in many Serbian-dominated villages, where the attitude seemed to be typified by this comment from a local resident on the day of the independence referendum: "We're prepared to fight . . . the referendum does not exist for us."[13]

The Croatian attitude on the legitimacy of the Serbian attempt at local self-determination was summed up by Stipe Mesic. As late as August, he still claimed that he was Yugoslavia's rightful President, although he sounded much more like a spokesman for the Croatian republic. At a press conference, Mesic advised that, "No negotiations about Croatian territories are possible with the Republic of Croatia," and that, "Control will be imposed by ways and means we will have to use in the areas where this control is not existent now."[14] This has turned out to mean civil war.

The Price of Intolerance

It is obvious that the cause of peace would have been much better served if the Serbs and Croats had each shown a minimum level of respect for the legitimate aspirations of the other side. Perhaps nobody could have avoided a civil war in an atmosphere so poisoned by hatred. Still, it seems that the federal government could have provided at least a hope of peace if it had taken some simple advance measures. It would have been wise to:

1. Admit the Inevitable

First and most critically, the federal government should have adopted some form of secession legislation in advance. It may seem self-destructive to adopt laws governing the splitting up of a country, since doing so gives legitimacy to the notion of separatism. However, this is better than the alternative, which is to have separation occur anyway, and turn violent due to the absence of any governing legislation.

History is full of examples of countries that lacked legal secession mechanisms and fought civil wars as a result. The United States, for example, lost 700,000 soldiers in its civil war. The fighting did not, as is commonly thought, begin on the issue of slavery, but over an attempt by the southern states to exercise a right of secession that had been implicit when those states had ratified the Constitution. Most of the wars of independence that have raged across the former European empires in Asia, Africa, and the Americas during the past two centuries have been the result of the lack of legal mechanisms for separation.

Provisions for local referenda on partition ought to have been built into Yugoslavia's separation law. Since it was clear from the start that Serbia would never consent to letting its hereditary enemy rule over any Serbian majority region, the law of the land should have reflected this fact. The existence of a legal framework would also have limited the ambitions of the Serbian minority, who now seem intent on killing or exiling every Croat who lives in the Serbian-majority regions of Croatia. A law of separation adopted in advance of the actual events might have prevented this.

2. Communicate Clearly

A second mistake made by the Serbians was to send mixed signals to the people of Croatia. Even in the midst of the most divisive political crises, tacit understandings can still be developed as long as both sides are sending clear messages. For instance, there was nothing confusing about Croatia's message to Serbia: We fear you and we want out of the Yugoslav federation because you increasingly dominate it.

Serbia's bottom line was never clear. In June, 1991, the actions of the Serbian-controlled federal military suggested that separation itself was unacceptable. When the Slovenian republic attempted to implement its declaration of independence in the early summer, it was met with organized military resistance from the federal army. For a brief period after this it seemed that control of border crossing points was Serbia's main concern. Only after several weeks had passed did Serbia change its focus, abandon its attacks on Slovenia, and attempt instead to secure the partition of Croatia on ethnic lines.

The confusing aggressiveness of Serbia's actions had made it impossible for Croatia to react in any way other than to fight every Serbian move. Even backing down quietly on the partition issue in the face of superior Serbian military strength was not an option, since the Croats could not be sure that once a Serbian victory had been attained on this issue, the Serbs would not attempt to press their advantages and seize all of Croatia.

LESSONS FOR CANADA

If Quebec is to be partitioned without the kind of violence that has taken place in Northern Ireland and Croatia, the lessons of these examples must be carefully analyzed. To be sure, Canada seems to present more promise than either Ireland or Yugoslavia ever did. French and English Canadians are not hereditary enemies, and the tradition of respecting democratic votes in this country is two centuries old. Even so, we can benefit by learning from the mistakes of others.

Lesson One: The Need for Partition Legislation

First, Canada needs to adopt legislation governing separation and partition. Adopting such legislation will not give added legitimacy to the notion of separatism. The fact is that all sectors of Canadian society already agree that the separation option is a right that should be granted (however reluctantly) to the province of Quebec.

What we have failed to mention is that in recognizing this right of self-determination without attaching any provisions to it, we are in effect telling Quebec that it may separate on its own terms and conditions. That Quebec has taken this message to heart is evidenced by some of the extreme proposals which were presented at the hearings of the Bélanger-Campeau Commission. If Quebec is presented at the last moment with Canada's real negotiating position, it will feel—not without justification—that Canada has been grossly dishonest in not making its bottom line clear from the start.

Canada has three choices in this matter:

- It can adopt legislation to govern separation and partition;

- It can allow Quebec to do the legislating on these matters for us, with predictable results as far as Canada's national interest is concerned; or

- It can take the Serbian approach and announce its terms and conditions at the last minute. There is no particular reason to think that this third approach will be any more effective here than it has been in Yugoslavia.

Lesson Two: Partition Must Take Place *Before Separation*

The approach attempted by the British in Northern Ireland involved negotiating a partition after the fact of Irish independence. It didn't work in Ireland, and it is equally unlikely to work in Canada unless what the federal government has in mind is to offer even more territory to Quebec without compensation, as recently suggested by Laval University professor Henri Brun.[15]

It is not enough to talk about partition in advance and then to try to carry out the act afterwards. The accession to sovereignty cements a country's hold on its territory—to partition it afterwards in the absence of its government's consent is both in law and in fact an act of war.

Lesson Three: Rely Only on Local Majority Wishes

The partitioning of Quebec must be done in a democratic manner, based solely on the concept of local sovereignty. The British technique of using a panel of arbitrators to sit in a small room and draw a new borderline on a map is less acceptable in a democratic country than a system based upon popular votes in individual districts. Judicial impartiality is almost impossible in matters such as these. The unenthusiastic reception received by the Irish Boundary

Commission's proposal demonstrates that getting all sides to agree to accept the validity of the decisions of such a commission is even more difficult. Only a system based upon popular votes will have a chance of legitimacy.

The failures in Ireland and Yugoslavia show that partition in Quebec can be based on one factor only: the principle of self-determination as expressed in local referenda. A partition which holds arable lands, sewage systems, and backyard boundaries to be more important than the desires of the inhabitants will be rejected as confusing and illegitimate.

Many partition plans that place physical assets ahead of popular wishes have been suggested for Quebec. Some proponents of partition have endorsed Quebec's right of self-determination, with the exception of the parts of the province that lie on the south shore of the St. Lawrence, which should be simply seized by the federal government to maintain a link with the eastern provinces. Others advocate the reclamation of the northern two-thirds of the province, to which Canada has a historical claim. The number of these exceptions to the principle of local self-determination have a tendency to grow, with the desires of the local inhabitants always coming last.

In both Croatia and Northern Ireland the advocates of partition recognized the importance of the principle of local majority rule, but they were unclear on the units within which majority self-rule would apply. This led to the obvious temptation for each side in each dispute to define the units of partition to its own best advantage. The choice of any unit of partition is arbitrary, but it is better to specify any units in advance than to specify none at all and fight about it afterwards.

Lesson Four: Incorporate the Separatists' Referendum Into the Partition Plan

The advocate of partition who seeks to carry out his plans peacefully is at a considerable disadvantage in that he must win the tacit co-operation of the citizens of the seceding nation, who have every reason to oppose partition. To do this, he must show respect for the separatists as they carry out their democratically-based secession. From this point of view, the boycott of the Croatia-wide referendum of May 19, 1991, by Croatia's Serbian minority was a tactical error. In Quebec, it will be particularly important to show respect for the province-wide referendum process. If the Quebec referendum is ridiculed by the advocates of partition (no matter how evasive the question posed by the provincial government) and a partition formula is developed which ignores its results, then it is hard to believe that the separatists could be persuaded to respect the partitionists' own local referenda. Besides, strongly corresponding votes in the tabulation of local returns from the province-wide referendum and from the various local referenda will be a strong indicator that these referenda were indeed fair, just, and democratically executed.

SUMMARY

History is a harsh teacher, as the experiences of Ireland and Yugoslavia demonstrate. Studying the cases of these two countries teaches us that partition plans fail when there is a general lack of respect of the democratic process, or when other concerns are set ahead of the will of the people who live in the regions that are being partitioned.

We learn from history that:

- **Partition legislation must be entrenched in the constitution.**
  It is vital that the government of a country acts under the umbrella of an existing law when it initiates the partitioning of a breakaway part of the state.

- **Partition must take place before separation occurs, not after.**
  To attempt a partition after separation has occurred means that a single legal system can no longer be used to govern the land transfer process. Since the only alternative to a law-based partition process is a process based on force, the dangers involved are as vast as the imagination.

- **Partition must be democratic.**
  The desires of the inhabitants of any given area must have priority over all other considerations, such as national security and the ownership of fixed assets.

- **The separatists must be involved in the partition process.**
  Involvement encourages participation and disarms attempts to stalemate or boycott the democratic partition process.

CHAPTER TWO

Partition in Switzerland: A Model for Canada

Most partitions throughout history have had unhappy conclusions, but there are exceptions. Switzerland has been, throughout its long and peaceful history, the site of four successful partitions. The canton of Appenzell was partitioned in 1597 as a way of ending religious strife that had driven the canton to the edge of civil war. Unterwalden was partitioned in stages between the fourteenth and nineteenth centuries. Basel was partitioned in 1833 as a result of severe urban-rural tensions. The canton of Jura was created in 1979 out of the northern region of Berne canton. A combination of religious and linguistic tensions made this partition necessary.

Only two of these partitions are relevant to the problem of partitioning Quebec. The Appenzell partition is interesting because it provides an almost exact parallel to Northern Ireland; it demonstrates how the Northern Ireland partition could have been handled more successfully. This in turn provides useful lessons which can be applied to Quebec. The story of the Jura partition is directly relevant to Quebec because of the similarity of the Jurassian separatist movement to the one in Quebec, and also because the partition formula which was applied in the Jura was remarkably effective in producing a peaceful and just solution to an incendiary situation.

THE APPENZELL PARTITION OF 1597

Appenzell in Context

Appenzell is a small canton in eastern Switzerland, located not far from Lake Constance and the German border. The canton joined the Swiss Confederation in 1513. The Confederation in those days was little more than a military alliance; Appenzell remained an independent republic both in name and in fact before joining and for many years afterward.

The canton had always been somewhat divided by its geography. The mountainous and isolated south-central region, known as 'Inner Rhodes,' was largely pastoral. Its residents depended mainly upon shepherding for their livelihood, but supplemented this by hiring out as mercenary soldiers. The Vatican City's Swiss Guards are a remnant of this era. The rest of the canton was known as 'Outer Rhodes.' By the time of the Reformation it had developed a textile industry and no longer depended upon warfare as a source of income. These economic factors were the cause of limited regional tensions in the early 1500s.

Church and State: The Twin Disintegrators

As the century progressed, the Reformation split the canton along religious lines. Most of the population of Inner Rhodes clung to the old religion, while the majority in Outer Rhodes enthusiastically adopted the Protestant teachings of Huldrych Zwingli. Vain attempts were made to reconcile the two faiths. The *Landsgemeinde*, or citizens' assembly, voted at first to let Protestants and Catholics preach alternately in each of the canton's communes. When this measure failed, it was decided that the question of religion should be left to individual communes. The result was poor treatment of religious minorities in all parts of the canton. A great debate between Zwingli and several learned Catholic doctors was planned in 1524, but it fell through when the Catholic community refused to sanction it.

By the 1580s, the religious split had brought Appenzell to the brink of civil war. Attempts were made to force minority residents in both parts of the canton to conform to the religious practices of the local majority. In May 1588 the entire Protestant population of the capital city removed themselves to the neighbouring town of Gais, where they could legally continue to practice their faith. On

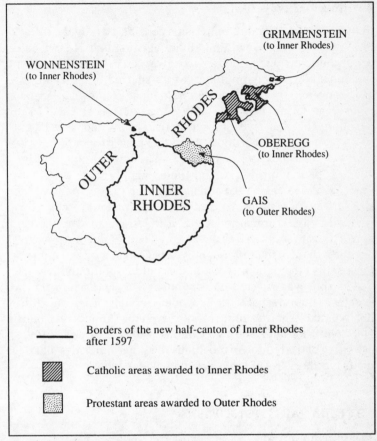

The Appenzell Partition of 1597. (Fig. 3)

another occasion a plot was discovered to murder all the Protestants of Inner Rhodes. The Protestants, meanwhile, had gained control of the Landsgemeinde and refused to appoint Catholics to any political office.

Finally, in 1596, leaders from Inner Rhodes proposed that the canton be divided on religious lines. Outer Rhodes agreed, and a boundary commission was established to partition the canton. The commissioners were selected entirely from other Swiss cantons. This made the commission impartial and may account for its success as compared to the Irish Boundary Commission.

Dividing the Spoils

In making its award, the commission considered only the factor of local majority wishes within individual communes. In two cases, communities in Outer Rhodes were awarded to Inner Rhodes, and one Inner Rhodes community was transferred to Outer Rhodes. Two convents were also transferred to Inner Rhodes. The enclaves of Oberegg, Grimmenstein, and Wonnenstein were created by this partition. These enclaves still exist today, nearly 400 years later.

The commission also divided up other assets: Inner Rhodes was to pay Outer Rhodes 10,000 guilder for its share of public buildings in the capital. Outside pension funds, mainly from the King of France, were to be divided equally between the two new cantons. Even the ownership of the contents of the national archives was decided by the commission. Inner Rhodes was to keep the great seal of the canton, as well as the captured battle flags of Appenzell's enemies. In turn, the representatives of Outer Rhodes were never to be denied the right of access to the contents of the archives.

The split was effected on September 8, 1597. Each of the two Rhodes became a separate, independent republic. Their only future link would be shared voting privileges on the Confederal Council. Four centuries later, the two cantons continue to peacefully co-exist, free of the burden of rebellious religious minorities that have made Northern Ireland into a perpetual war zone.

THE JURA PARTITION OF 1979

The Jura in Context

The region known as the Jura, in northern Switzerland, has been a canton since 1979. Before this, it had been part of the canton of Berne since the end of the Napoleonic wars. Before 1792, the Jura was an ecclesiastic principality and an independent state in its own right, a status it had held since 999 AD. Berne, too, was at one time an independent country. Today both areas are Swiss cantons, with roughly the same legal status as Canadian provinces.

The partition of the Jura region is notable for the peaceful and civilized handling of a difficult and volatile situation. Of all the available partition models, it is the one which is most likely to be compatible with the avoidance of civil strife and the preservation of good relations between Quebec and English Canada. Even though the Jura separation did not involve the creation of a new independent nation-state, the parallels between the Jura and Quebec are remarkable—so much so that Jean LaPierre, the deputy leader of the Bloc Québécois, has stated that he regards the Jurassian secessionist party, the *Rassemblement jurassien*, as the model for his new party.

Like Quebec, the Jura region is mainly francophone (Berne is mostly German), but is also home to a large population of non-francophones. These are mostly German speakers whose ancestors had settled in the region long after the original French-speaking population. Like the anglophone population of Quebec, the German minority is concentrated largely in urban areas. There are also several smaller German-majority rural districts. One particularly large German-populated rural district called 'Laufen' is very similar (in its thoroughly non-francophone character and its total isolation from the rest of the German-speaking parts of Berne) to the Eastern Townships of southern Quebec.

The Jura region is also home to a large population of French-speaking Protestants who historically have shown far less enthusiasm for secession than their French Catholic neighbours.

The Referenda of 1974-75

In 1974, after years of separatist agitation, the population of the Jura region held a referendum on secession.

Switzerland has a long-standing tradition of democratic change. The challenge faced by Bernese officials was to ensure that the democratic rights of the germanophone and French Protestant minorities would be protected should the Jura region vote to separate. In 1970, they passed legislation to govern the handling of secession referenda. One provision of this legislation allowed local majorities in individual districts of the Jura region to choose to remain part of Berne.

The referendum process consisted of three rounds of voting. In the first round on June 23, 1974, all voters in the Jura region were asked, simply, *Voulez-vous constituer un nouveau canton?* (Do you want to create a new canton?)[16] An overall majority of 52 percent of Jurassian voters favoured secession. This included majorities in three of the region's seven districts. Majorities in the remaining four districts, however, rejected the separatist option by margins ranging from 57 to over 90 percent. The overall pro-separation vote

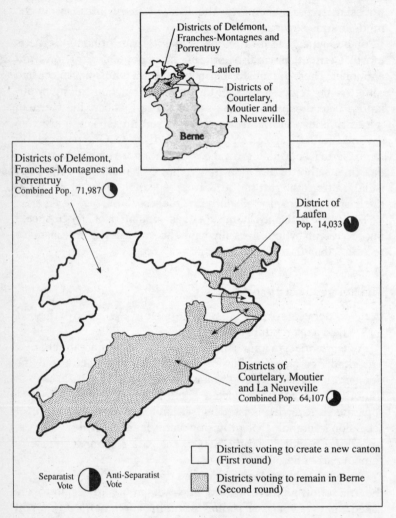

Districts of Delémont,
Franches-Montagnes and
Porrentruy

Laufen

Districts of
Courtelary,
Moutier and
La Neuveville

Berne

Districts of Delémont,
Franches-Montagnes and
Porrentruy
Combined Pop. 71,987

District of
Laufen
Pop. 14,033

Districts of
Courtelary, Moutier
and La Neuveville
Combined Pop. 64,107

Separatist
Vote

Anti-Separatist
Vote

Districts voting to create a new canton
(First round)

Districts voting to remain in Berne
(Second round)

1st and 2nd rounds of voting in the Jura. (Fig. 4)

set in motion two additional rounds of voting before it became clear just where the new cantonal borderline would be located.

The second referendum took place only in the districts that had chosen to vote against the creation of a new canton. It was clear from the results of the first vote that the new Jurassian canton would include the territory of the three districts which had voted for secession. The voters in the districts loyal to Berne were therefore given the option of reconsidering their votes, to enable them to join the new canton. In each case, majorities chose to remain in Berne.

In the third round, individual municipalities in all districts were given the opportunity to secede from Berne and join the Jura, or vice versa. Eight municipalities voted to join the new canton, while two others voted to leave it and rejoin Berne. The end result of all this voting was that the new canton of Jura contained a little over half the territory and population of the old Jura region.

Local majorities were respected in all situations except where unworkably small enclaves of Bernese land would have been left in the midst of Jurassian territory, or the reverse. Thanks to the careful planning of the referendum formula, majority votes only had to be overruled in four tiny municipalities with a combined population of 537.

The End Result

Today the Jura region is a separate canton, fully equal to Berne and to each of Switzerland's twenty-two other cantons. Its population is almost entirely French-speaking; there is no significant German minority to object to the canton's vigorous efforts to promote the French language and culture.

Most encouraging of all, the entire process of secession and partition took place in an atmosphere of peace, if not of actual goodwill. Previously Jurassian separatism had been marked by considerable hostility and even by terrorism, sponsored by the alarmingly familiar sounding *Front de liberation jurassien*, or FLJ. Beginning in 1962, the FLJ had launched a terrorist campaign involving attacks on military installations, railways, and Protestant farmsteads, but it fell silent as the separatists turned their efforts instead to garnering support for each round of voting in the referendum process. The terrorist movement has never been revived.

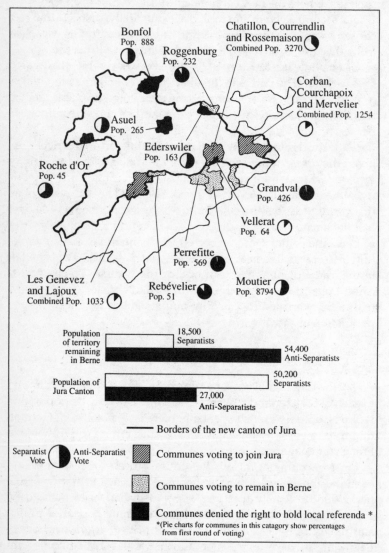

Bonfol
Pop. 888

Roggenburg
Pop. 232

Chatillon, Courrendlin
and Rossemaison
Combined Pop. 3270

Corban,
Courchapoix
and Mervelier
Combined Pop. 1254

Asuel
Pop. 265

Ederswiler
Pop. 163

Roche d'Or
Pop. 45

Grandval
Pop. 426

Vellerat
Pop. 64

Perrefitte
Pop. 569

Les Genevez
and Lajoux
Combined Pop. 1033

Rebévelier
Pop. 51

Moutier
Pop. 8794

Population
of territory
remaining
in Berne

18,500
Separatists

54,400
Anti-Separatists

Population of
Jura Canton

50,200
Separatists

27,000
Anti-Separatists

—— Borders of the new canton of Jura

Separatist
Vote   Anti-Separatist
Vote

Communes voting to join Jura

Communes voting to remain in Berne

Communes denied the right to hold local referenda *
*(Pie charts for communes in this catagory show percentages
from first round of voting)

3rd round of voting in the Jura. (Fig. 5)

THE SECRET OF PEACEFUL PARTITION

How the Jurassian Separatists Became Active Partitionists

One of the most intriguing things about the partition process adopted by the Bernese authorities is the way in which it forced the Jurassian separatists to participate actively in the partition process. Initially the separatist leadership had demanded that the region be permitted to separate as a single territorial unit, regardless of the wishes of German and French-Protestant minorities in its various localities.

In some ways the leadership of the Rassemblement jurassien was more extreme than its Québécois equivalent. Until 1973, the party opposed the concept of a referendum altogether, even though it had sponsored an unsuccessful plebiscite on separation in 1959. As well, the Rassemblement boycotted the legislative debates on the alternatives to separation, and refused to participate when a commission of inquiry, called the 'Commission de 24,' was established by the cantonal government to study the Jura problem. In 1970, when the legislation permitting the Jura to hold a referendum was written into the Bernese constitution, the Rassemblement threatened to wreck the referendum process. As a condition of co-operation, it demanded that the right to vote be denied to all residents of the Jura who could not trace their ancestry within the region back at least ninety years.

This demand was clearly designed to disenfranchise German-speaking immigrants and children of immigrants, who were likely to vote against separation in the first round of balloting and in favour of partition in subsequent rounds. It was an openly anti-democratic demand offensive to Swiss sensibilities, and it gained little support among the French Catholic grassroots elements to whom the separatists were appealing. Unable to rouse popular sentiments against the multi-stage referendum process, the separatists found that once they had set the referendum machinery in motion by calling a region-wide referendum on separation, they were forced to battle for votes in the local referenda or else risk losing additional territory to the Bernese. Their resultant participation gave legitimacy to the whole multiple-referendum process and made it impossible to stir up a large scale organized effort to oppose partitioning.

Some observers of the Jura partition have been inclined to find the secret of its success in Switzerland's long democratic tradition.

There is some value in this observation; certainly the habit of respecting the outcome of referenda seems to be more deeply ingrained among the Swiss than among the Serbs and Croats. To most Swiss, the idea of taking any serious political action without first consulting the people through a binding referendum is inconceivable. One can only hope that French and English Canadians, with two centuries of democracy behind them, will react with equal respect for democracy if the Jura formula is applied in this country.

In addition to this factor, there are three reasons why the Jura partition was a success where the Irish and Croatian partitions were not. Each of these reasons relates to the legislation governing the referendum and separation process which was followed in the Jura.

LESSONS FOR CANADA

Lesson One: Prepare A Partition Law in Advance

First, the very fact of the existence of legislation governing the separation of the Jura was a strong factor in maintaining the peace. The whole process of separation and partition was governed by the rule of law. In any crisis situation where large groups of people have different and conflicting goals, the only alternative to the rule of law is the rule of the strong over the weak, through implied violence or else by naked force. This had been the unhappy discovery of the citizens of Croatia and Nagorno-Karabakh, where partitions have been attempted in the absence of a legal framework.

The legislation governing Jurassian separation and partition was proposed in November 1968 and adopted as an amendment to the Bernese cantonal constitution by means of a canton-wide referendum held in 1970. After this, the rules governing any future separation were clearly defined and all sides were aware of the alternatives: they could either play by these rules or attempt to subvert them by illegal means or by non-participation. Attempts to redefine the rules were notably unsuccessful. The Rassemblement jurassien's attempt to disenfranchise the Jura's germanophones was one such attempt. One indication of the success of the new constitutional amendments in redefining the terms of the separation debate is the fact that even this attempt at disruption was forced to take the existing legislation as its starting point. To do otherwise would have rendered the attempt so irrelevant to the debate that it would have had no meaning at all.

The reason why the constitutional amendments of 1970 were so effective in changing the terms of the separation debate was that the new law was fair, generous, and even-handed, but also tough-minded. The terms it spelled out for the conduct of local referenda were identical to the ones used for the Jura-wide referendum. The questions which would be asked in each round of voting—"Do you want to create a new canton?" and "Do you want our commune to continue to be part of the canton of Berne?"—were straightfor-ward, especially as compared to the question posed in Quebec's 1980 referendum, which contained 108 words and three semico-lons. This made the Swiss referendum legislation very difficult to attack on grounds of principle.

Lesson Two: Vote at the Local Level

The legislation governing the Jura partition was also very specific in its delimitation of the areas in which local referenda could be held. This prevented the sort of drawn-out and pointless debates which raged in the meeting rooms of the Irish Boundary Commis-sion over the proper size of an 'area' in which local inhabitants would be able to decide their own fate, or whether one-vote major-ities ought to count.

In the Jura, single-vote majorities were considered to be a per-fectly acceptable indication of the will of the populace. (No one-vote majorities were recorded, although there was a tie vote in the commune of Bonfol.)

As for delimiting regions in which votes would be held, the Bernese took the concept of local self-determination to its logical conclusion. The right was extended to the smallest existing politi-cal units, the communes. In Switzerland, the commune is the equivalent of the Canadian township; it is the main organ of municipal government. In the Jura, nearly 100 communes had populations of less than 1,000. Of these, thirteen had less than 100 residents at the time of the 1970 census. The smallest commune to exercise its right of self-determination was a rural community named Rebévelier, with a population of fifty-one and an electorate of only three dozen individuals. In a local referendum held in the fall of 1975, the residents of this tiny community voted to secede from the district of Delémont in the new Jura canton and join the district of Moutier, which remained in Berne.

The Jura experience showed two things: one, that very tiny

populations are capable of exercising the right of self-determination in an orderly manner; and two, that referenda are far less
divisive when they are held in very small areas than when they are
conducted in large regions. The largest commune to conduct a local
referendum in the autumn of 1975 was the town of Moutier,
administrative centre of the district of the same name. The population of the town of Moutier at that time was 8,800. In the Jura-wide
referendum of the previous year, 49 percent of its voters had cast
their ballots in favour of separation. As the date of the local referendum approached, activists from both sides of the separation
issue descended upon the town.

What happened next is described in a brief presented to the
Swiss Federal Chamber of Deputies by representatives of the Jura's
anti-separatists:

> Between June 24 and the date of the vote, many citizens of
> northern Jura [the separatist heartland] tried to get themselves
> registered on the town's electoral rolls . . . . From the 1st to the
> 8th of September 1975, the town was occupied by separatist
> demonstrators who tried to intimidate the partisans of Berne,
> to keep them from freely expressing their views and to make
> the populace feel that if it did not submit, it would never be able
> to enjoy peace and tranquillity. It was necessary to bring in a
> sizable police contingent to re-establish order. These last had
> already intervened once on April 24, when, in violation of a
> municipal ban on demonstrations, separatists rioted causing
> vandalism, broken windows, damaged cars and injuries.[17]

The Moutier riots caused no fatalities, but on one occasion ten
policemen were seriously injured. As Kenneth McRae writes in his
book on Swiss ethnic relations, these tactics left such a bad taste in
everybody's mouth that "since 1975 Moutier has remained in-
tensely polarized at the level of shops, cafés, businesses and even
within families, and the militant separatist youth movement, the
Béliers [Battering Rams] has produced an equally action-oriented
anti-separatist counterpart, the Sangliers [Wild Boars]."[18]

The high pressure atmosphere of Moutier was a striking contrast
to the relatively laid-back situation in Rebévelier and the other
small communes. The tension in Moutier was the result of the
stakes involved: the fate of an entire administrative and industrial
centre rested upon a few dozen swing votes. Militants on either

side of the separation issue were willing to use whatever tactics they could dream up to make the vote go in their favour.

The Moutier story is particularly unnerving when one remembers that in the Quebec context, Moutier is just a small town. The city of Montreal is the largest municipality in Quebec; its population is 115 times as large as the commune of Moutier. There are many other Quebec cities and towns considerably larger than Moutier where the voters are likely to be just as evenly divided as they were in that town.

This suggests that the logical approach in Quebec would be to carry out local referenda in political divisions smaller than the province's municipalities. In Chapter Four, I will suggest that local referenda be held on the level of the poll, or *section de vote*, which was the most local level on which votes were calculated in the 1980 referendum.

Lesson Three: The Sole Focus Must Be On Self-Determination

Another factor in the success of the Jura partition process was the single-minded focus of the governing legislation on the goal of local self-determination. In contrast to the Irish Boundary Commission with its long list of conditions, the Bernese constitutional amendments of 1970 on separation and partition had only one goal: to maximize the ability of individuals to choose the canton in which they would live. Despite the best efforts of the Rassemblement jurassien, this goal was communicated quite effectively to the grassroots French Catholic population which was the real force behind the Jurassian separatist movement.

This is an important lesson for those who feel Quebec should surrender more than just its non-francophone regions. There are those who insist that Quebec should give up territory on historical, legal, or strategic grounds. It is important to realize that it will be impossible to justify these concerns to the francophones of Quebec. In attempting to excise French-majority regions from the province, we would, in essence, be telling the Québécois to respect the right of self-determination for English speakers and Natives, even though the same right would be denied to many francophones.

The final lesson for Canada, therefore, is to be sure that any legislation governing the partitioning of Quebec includes no limitations on local self-determination, whether these be founded on concerns over law, history, security, or any other secondary or tertiary factors. The primary concern must be to uphold the right of individuals within each community to decide their own fate.

SUMMARY

The Swiss examples show that there are three essential elements in achieving peaceful and democratic partition. These are:

- **Institute a partition plan in advance.**
  Entrench the partition plan in the constitution. This validates the process and better ensures the participation of citizens in referendum votes. Legislating the means of departure from a federation does not justify the act of secession; it merely rationalizes the process in the event that separation should occur.

- **Conduct voting at the most local level possible.**
  The idea in partitioning is to give as many people as possible the chance to live in the country of their choice. The smaller the voting units in a partition referendum, the more people can become enfranchised in the country to which they feel they belong.

- **The focus must be on self-determination only.**
  The idea is that local self-determination is the only method by which people can be assured the right to live in the country of their choice. Other considerations, such as historical, legal, and strategic concerns, or the ownership of fixed capital assets in the territory to be partitioned, are not nearly as important from a humane point of view.

CHAPTER THREE

A Few "Modest Proposals": A History of Partitionist Ideas in Canada

Jonathan Swift wrote his famous *Modest Proposal* in 1789 to mock the ridiculous schemes of many English critics of Ireland. Swift argued most convincingly that the English should eat Irish babies to keep the population down.

If Swift were alive in Canada today, he might have satirized the impractical plans of Canadian partitionists. Many disturbing partition proposals have been put forward over the past three decades. Unfortunately, none of them are intended to be satirical.

SIX PARTITION PROPOSALS

The Brossard Proposal (1976)

Québécois nationalists are notoriously unenthusiastic about discussing the possibility of partition. Parti Québécois leader Jacques Parizeau, for example, has repeatedly stated that under Canadian law, no province's boundaries may be altered without the consent of that province. Once the province has become an independent country, Parizeau's argument continues, its borders will be protected by international law.

Parti Québécois vice-president Bernard Landry gives another reason why partition is unacceptable to the nationalists: self-determination is a right reserved to peoples, or 'nations,' like the Québécois. Quebec's minorities do not constitute nations, hence they do not have the right to self-determination. Referring to talk of excising Montreal's English-majority West Island from an independent Quebec, Landry delivered what he considered to be the ultimate put-down: "I've never seen any mention of a West Island nation."[19]

Both Parizeau and Landry have been drawing their ideas from the writings of Jacques Brossard, a professor of law at the University of Montreal and a constitutional expert for the Parti Québécois. Brossard's 1976 book, *L'accession à la souveraineté et le cas du Québec*, contains the most extensive discussion of partition from a nationalist point of view to be found anywhere. Brossard uses the national self-determination argument as a basis for rejecting partition. French Canadians, he insists, qualify as "a people" under the charter of the United Nations, and therefore Quebec, as their sole political representative, possesses the right of self-determination which the charter accords to all nation-states.[20] The same right does not extend to Quebec's minorities, since none of them qualify as "a people" in just the right way.

For instance, Quebec's anglophones are disqualified because they are part of a larger "people" that Brossard calls "the English Canadian Nation."[21] The existence of an independent Canada means that the anglophones of Quebec already have a nation-state of their own. In Brossard's interpretation, this means that English-speaking Quebecers already have everything to which they are entitled under the United Nations charter. The fact that they would have to uproot themselves in order to live in their national homeland, or that they might lose their Canadian passports in an independent Quebec, does not strike Professor Brossard as being a limitation upon this right.

Brossard displays a reluctant willingness to discuss the possibility of partition, but only for "heavily anglophone regions along Quebec's borders."[22] As a guideline, he suggests that even along the borders, areas should only be allowed to secede if the local anglophone majority is 80 percent or more because "that's the same majority as francophones have in Quebec as a whole."[23] Under Brossard's twin criteria, only a few small municipalities in Pontiac County west of Ottawa, a single township just south of Labrador, and a pair of tiny islands in the Magdalen Islands archipelago in the Gulf of St. Lawrence would be eligible to secede from Quebec. The total population of these areas is perhaps one half of one percent of Quebec's total non-francophone population.

In return for this generosity, Brossard feels that Canada should reopen discussions of the Labrador boundary issue, and should be willing to consider ceding territorial waters in Hudson's Bay and land in New Brunswick to a sovereign Quebec.[24]

Brossard's proposals are clearly unacceptable to most Canadians, but they provide a useful contrast to the partition proposals coming out of English Canada, and show just how vast the gulf is between the two points of view.

A surprisingly large number of proposals for slicing up Quebec have been put forth. Given the sensitivity that francophone Quebec feels toward the partition issue, it is disturbing to observe how incendiary and poorly thought out some of these partition proposals are. Others are well reasoned, but none takes the lessons of history's previous partitions into account, and therefore none of them is actually suited to practical implementation.

The Albert-Shaw Proposal (1980)

The most influential partition plan is set forth by Lionel Albert and William Shaw in their 1980 book, *Partition: The Price of Quebec's Independence*. Albert and Shaw argue that if Quebec attempts to gain independence, it should be deprived of about 80 percent of its territory. Quebec's legal claim to most of this land, they believe, is founded solely upon the province's continued participation in Confederation. If Quebec were to secede, it would forfeit its right to control the northern two-thirds of its landmass, as well as all lands south of the St. Lawrence River. Extensive legal and historical arguments are set forth in support of these claims.

The authors also call for Canada to assume control of certain other areas of the province—the Outaouais, all of Montreal west of St-Denis Street, and the north coast of the Gulf of St. Lawrence—on the grounds that these areas contain sizable non-francophone minorities and considerable numbers of pro-Federalist francophones. One result of the plan is that more francophones would remain in Canada than in the truncated Republic of Quebec.

Probably the most important thing to remember about the Albert-Shaw partition plan is that it is never meant to take place. By warning Quebecers that a partition plan would be part of any separation agreement, Albert and Shaw hope to deflate the nationalist contention that Quebec can secede without suffering any negative consequences. They write, " . . . a country will not be proclaimed—ever. The French-Canadian people would not have it.

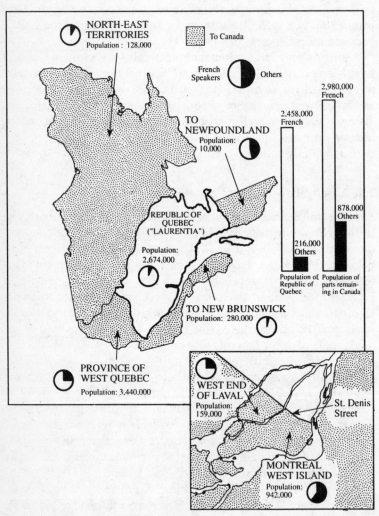

The Albert-Shaw Proposal, 1980. (Fig. 6)

They would rather have a large province than a small country. That is why separation will not happen."[25]

Perhaps this conclusion would have been justified if federalist politicians had possessed the courage to bring the partition issue into the open before the nationalists seized control of Quebec's political agenda in early 1991 with the Allaire and Bélanger-Campeau reports. As a discussion point in the early stages of the post-Meech debate, the Albert-Shaw plan could have been one of the most useful tools at the disposal of the federalists. As an actual plan for partition, however, it is both impractical and dangerous.

My own discussions with Lionel Albert suggest that as separation has become a more realistic possibility, he has moderated his position on some territorial proposals, with the intent of making them more suitable to practical application. The details of these plans have not yet been published.

The McDonald Proposal (1990)

Much of what has been said about the Albert-Shaw plan can be repeated for the proposal presented by Kenneth McDonald in his book, *Keeping Canada Together*. McDonald argues that if English Canada were to insist upon a particularly harsh form of partition as a condition of Quebec's independence, the separatists would be forced to back down and accept renewed federalism as a more palatable alternative. This may explain why, in strictly territorial terms, McDonald's is the harshest partition plan ever put forth. In the passage below, he describes the boundaries that he would grant to an independent Quebec:

> Without Rupert's Land, without land access to the United States save through Canadian territory, Quebec would be little more than an island state: Montreal, plus a quadrilateral roughly 650 miles by 250. Its borders would be approximately a line running northwest from Montreal island to a point south of Val d'Or and east of Temiskaming, northeast from there to Wabush, and then south to the north shore of the St. Lawrence. Such a sovereign Quebec might still be economically viable— as Singapore is, as Taiwan is—but it's unlikely to appeal to many Quebecers when the alternative is to retain all of its present territory, and much of its present quasi-sovereignty, within the Canadian framework.[26]

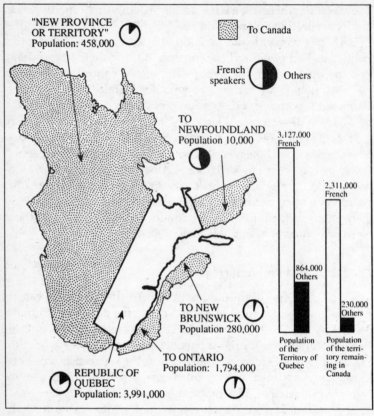

The McDonald Proposal, 1991. (Fig. 7)

The description above and the maps he includes in his book seem
to suggest that McDonald would not include any part of the island of
Montreal in the territory to be excised from Quebec. This is peculiar,
given that the majority of the province's non-francophones live there.
If actually implemented, McDonald's plan would result in an odd
situation in which over 40 percent of Quebec's francophones would
live on Canadian soil after separation, but only 20 percent of the
province's non-francophones would do so. As a result, the size of
Quebec's non-francophone community would grow from its present
16 percent to 22 percent following independence.

The "new province or territory" which McDonald proposes to
create out of Quebec's north and the Outaouais region would be 86
percent francophone—which is to say, slightly more homoge-

neously French-speaking than the province of Quebec is today, and substantially more homogeneous than the Republic of Quebec would be under his plan.

Both the McDonald proposal and the Albert-Shaw plan call for some of Quebec's territory to be awarded to New Brunswick. Their maps are a bit unclear on the exact extent of New Brunswick's territorial gains. If one assumes that the province would be awarded only those parts of Quebec that lie south of the St. Lawrence River and east of New Brunswick's westernmost point, the result is that the province would gain 280,000 new residents, 95 percent of whom are French-speaking. This influx would be sufficient to reduce New Brunswick's anglophones to minority status within their own province. This territory is a gift which New Brunswick might be reluctant to accept.

All of this suggests that, like the Albert-Shaw proposal, the plan set forth in *Keeping Canada Together* was meant to serve as a warning only, rather than as an actual blueprint for partition.

The Bercuson-Cooper Proposal (1991)

In its essentials, the partition plan proposed by David Jay Bercuson and Barry Cooper in their recent book, *Deconfederation: Canada Without Quebec*, is similar to the Albert-Shaw plan, upon which it appears to be based. Bercuson and Cooper differ from Albert and Shaw mainly in what appears to be a slightly more moderate position on the ownership of Montreal, the Outaouais, and the north shore of the Gulf of St. Lawrence. On the question of sovereignty over Quebec's north and of the south shore of the St. Lawrence River, they support precisely the same position as Albert and Shaw, on the basis of exactly the same arguments.

The most substantial difference between the Albert-Shaw plan and the proposals set out in *Deconfederation* is that Bercuson and Cooper are entirely serious about trying to impose their plan upon Quebec. They write, "Shaw and Albert [argue] that the French of Quebec would prefer a large province to a small country. *Perhaps they would. We, however, believe that the rest of us would be better off if Quebec were a small country and not a large province.*"[27]

This aggressive note is pursued throughout their discussion of partition. Faced with the problem that it might not be legally possible to effect a partition within the Canadian constitutional framework, the authors declare:

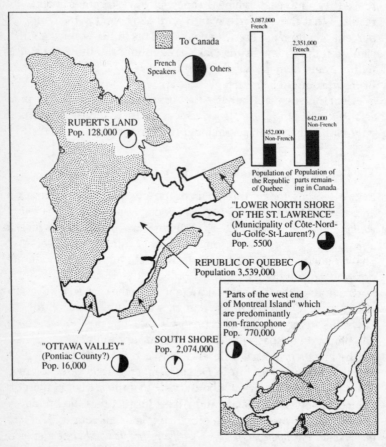

Bercuson-Cooper Proposal, 1991. (Fig. 8)

It is necessary, therefore, to resort to extra-constitutional procedures. This is a very serious step to take because it amounts
to something like a revolutionary founding or re-founding of
the regime. Not only has such an act never been taken in
Canadian history, but much of our history has been devoted to
the rejection of such acts. . . . But in the absence of international
and national legal procedures it would seem we have no choice
but to invent our own.[28]

Aside from the dubious contention that Canada cannot legally
conduct a partition, this argument invalidates the legalistic arguments on which Bercuson and Cooper base Canada's claim to most
of Quebec's territory. It is illogical to use legalistic historical claims
to justify the openly *illegal* seizure of territory. Democratic or
popular justifications are also clearly not relevant to the authors,
since most of the territory they would like to retain within Canada's
borders has a sizable francophone majority. All that is left is the use
of police or military strength, or at least the threat thereof, to
enforce an openly unconstitutional action.

Turning to the question of non-francophones residing in what is
left of Quebec after Rupert's Land and the South Shore have been
removed by force, Bercuson and Cooper indicate that Canada
should make "other territorial adjustments" in order to retain parts
of the Outaouais, the north shore of the Gulf of St. Lawrence, and
the west end of the Island of Montreal. "The political principle to
be invoked here," they explain, "is that if the French claim, on
ethnic and cultural grounds, a right to secede from Canada, then
the non-French have the right to secede from Quebec. What is sauce
for the goose is sauce for the gander."[29]

Invoking an equal right to self-determination on behalf of a
million non-francophones when they have just denied it to over
two million French-speaking Quebecers is a reflection of either
hypocrisy or intellectual confusion. The Bercuson-Cooper proposal
is no more than a new version, played a few octaves higher, of the old
discredited argument that the only way to handle those naughty
separatists is to tell them once and for all that their province will not
be permitted to separate, period. Just how all this territory, which
contains over two million francophones and presumably more than a
few militant separatists capable of constructing a pipe bomb, would
be excised from Quebec and rejoined to Canada is not explored in
Bercuson and Cooper's book.

The Robertson Proposal (1991)

The most alarming partition proposal currently in circulation is one recently set forth by Ian Ross Robertson, a professor at the University of Toronto. Robertson briefly addresses the question of Quebec's north and of the province's anglophone-majority areas, but his real interest is in the establishment of a corridor of Canadian territory between Ontario and New Brunswick. He provides detailed plans for the development of such a corridor. It would not occupy the entire South Shore, since, he acknowledges, the region has a large population of francophones. On the other hand, he insists that a corridor would have to be wide enough to provide a secure buffer zone around Canada's road and rail lines. In his estimation, a width of thirty to fifty kilometres would be necessary.

The precise location of the corridor is a problem:

> It could be either along the American border, thus depriving independent Quebec of adjacency to the United States, or elsewhere through the southern portion of the present province of Quebec. The latter will probably be at least as objectionable to Quebecers, for its effect would be the division of Quebec into two sections, one north and one south of the corridor.[30]

In the end Robertson opts for a strip along the American border as "the best solution for both Quebec and the rest of Canada." Assuming that the corridor is kept as close as possible to the 30-kilometre width that Robertson considers to be the minimum acceptable, it would contain 504,000 francophones. This makes his next proposal seem particularly disturbing:

> Persons living within the corridor would be required to elect allegiance to Canada or to Quebec. If the latter, they would have to move unless their presence in the corridor were deemed an asset to Canada; those required to move would be compensated, jointly by Quebec and by Canada, for their immovable assets.[31]

This sounds alarmingly like the British demand for an oath of allegiance that led to the deportation of the Acadians in the 1750s. Even in a best-case scenario, the results of such a policy would be disastrous. Assuming that only a 10 percent minority of the francophone population refused to swear loyalty to Canada, Robertson's plan would still lead to more than 50,000 deportations. This would be by far the largest deportation in Canadian history: larger by a factor of four than the deportation of the Acadians, more than twice as large as the forced relocation of the Japanese in 1942.

Robertson suggests that Canada and Quebec could negotiate the details of the corridor arrangement. More likely, his plan would have the two states at daggers drawn. Quebec would now have a vested interest in the rupture of Canada's eastern and western halves, since this might bring about the return of its lost corridor. The very least retaliation that could be expected from Quebec would be a severing of the existing transportation lines across its territory. No major road or rail lines presently lie entirely within the proposed corridor, leaving Canada completely sundered, at least for the short term, by a hostile state. For these reasons, we should dismiss Robertson's proposal.

The Varty Proposal (1991)

Considerably more sophisticated than the Bercuson-Cooper or Robertson proposals is a discussion put forth by Vancouver lawyer David Varty in a slim volume entitled *Who Gets Ungava?* Varty's discussion takes the form of a legal brief. He examines the wording of the *Act respecting the north-western, northern and north-eastern boundaries of the province of Quebec* of 1898 and the *Quebec Boundary Extension Act* of 1912, as well as the meaning in law of the concept of sovereignty. His conclusion is that Quebec would have no legal claim to the two sizable pieces of territory that were transferred to it in 1898 and 1912.

Varty therefore favours the transfer of this territory to Canadian federal jurisdiction in the event of a 'Yes' vote in a referendum on independence. He also proposes permitting the francophone-majority region in the extreme south of this vast area to join an independent Quebec, on the condition that Canada be financially compensated for the loss of this territory. Varty's plan is intended for actual implementation, and he spends some time elaborating how this could be done within the framework not only of Canadian law, but also of the referendum legislation now in place in Quebec.

Varty's proposal is a refreshing change from the others; it tries to be reasonable. He suggests acting on partition within a legal framework, while most others seem to propose illegal seizures of territory. Nevertheless, Varty bases his entire argument on the

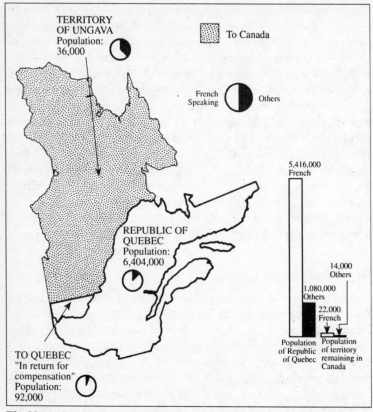

TERRITORY
OF UNGAVA
Population:
36,000

To Canada

French
Speaking   Others

5,416,000
French

14,000
Others

1,080,000
Others

22,000
French

REPUBLIC OF
QUEBEC
Population:
6,404,000

Population   Population
of Republic   of territory
of Quebec   remaining in
                Canada

TO QUEBEC
"In return for
compensation"
Population:
92,000

The Varty Proposal, 1991. (Fig. 9)

assumption that Quebec will leave Canada *and* the British Crown.
If Quebec remained a dominion of the Crown, as Ireland did in
1921, it would retain its sovereign right to Ungava.

Other Proposals

Many much sketchier partition proposals have been suggested in
the decade and a half since separation began to look like a real
possibility in the mid-1970s. Most have been much less thorough
than those outlined above and therefore are not reproduced here in
detail. The distinguished historian Donald Creighton produced a
proposal in a March 1977 article in *Maclean's*. Around the same
time, D.K. Donnelly published a book advocating the annexation
of Canada to the United States, but not before Quebec had been

expelled from Confederation and all non-francophone areas re-joined to Canada or the nearest American state, as appropriate.[32] Also in the 1970s, a 'Preparatory Committee for an Eleventh Province' was established to advocate the secession of non-franco-phone parts of Quebec and the formation of a new, genuinely bilingual province. Its work has been renewed in the 1990s by the Option Canada Party.

Regional partitionist movements have also existed on and off in Quebec's north, in the Eastern Townships, and in Pontiac County west of Ottawa-Hull. In Pontiac County, pressures in favour of partition have come in three waves, corresponding to the im-plementation of Bill 22 in 1972, the referendum of 1980, and the current referendum crisis. The tenacity of some of these local movements suggests they will be hard to ignore in the lead-up to the next referendum.

THE THREE LINES OF THOUGHT ON PARTITIONING

Aside from the Quebec nationalist contention that partition is impossible, there are three lines of thought on the subject. The first holds that Quebec has a legal or historical right only to part of its territory and that upon separation it must return to Canada all lands which historically belong to Canada. The second line of thought maintains that the key to the partition issue is national security; therefore, the main focus of any partition plan must be the maintenance of an all-Canadian corridor for road and rail traffic and other forms of communication between Ontario and New Bruns-wick. The third line of thought states that the same principle of local majority rule that the separatists have applied to Quebec as a whole ought to be applied to each locality within Quebec. Each of these smaller areas would have the right to determine whether it will remain in Canada or join the newly independent Quebec state.

Canadians should realize that following the partition plans set forth by the advocates of either of the first two schools of thought would involve tests of the national will that English Canada would probably not be able to successfully withstand. These plans involve the seizure of territory where the population has no interest in remaining part of Canada, and would ultimately lead to irredentism and terrorist violence. Following these plans would also involve abandoning the principle of individual and local-majority choice, which accurately reflects the core beliefs of most English Canadians, adopting instead some sort of principle based upon force.

If any force-based solution to the territorial issue is to be adopted, Canadians will need a new ideology. Perhaps a variant of the Quebec nationalist position could be taken up: Canada is a nation, and as such its existing borders (or whatever borders it chooses) are sacrosanct. Any rival nationalism, be it Québécois, Native, or otherwise, is illegitimate and may be dealt with by whatever means are most appropriate to the maintenance of the territorial integrity of the Canadian nation, including military occupation and overt violence. The problem with this sort of ideology is that nobody in Canada could be made to believe it.

1. Legal / Historical Arguments for Partition

Viewed from one angle, Canada's potential future border problems with Quebec are nothing more than a classic boundary dispute. Canada has had a number of such disputes in the past, usually with the United States. The poorly defined Maine border was settled in 1842 by the Webster-Ashburton Treaty. Disputes have also developed over the ownership of the Oregon Territory, the Alaska Panhandle, and islands in the Straits of Juan de Fuca. On each occasion, both sides presented eloquent legalistic and historically-based arguments in favour of their claims, and then settled for compromise solutions which reflected the relative strength and political will of the disputants, rather than any historical justice.

My opinion is that in the case of Quebec we should move directly to the compromise solution while there is still time to link it to such other factors as peace, local self-determination, and continued economic interaction between Canada and Quebec. Determined efforts to pursue legal claims to disputed territory have a long history of causing very unhappy outcomes, including wars.

Still, the historically-based arguments for partition are far more popular at present than any solution based upon democracy, and therefore they need to be explored.

Canada's Claim to the North

The most popular of the historically-based arguments is that Quebec should be able to take out of Confederation only the territory that it brought with it in 1867. The province's boundaries were extended to the north in 1898 and again in 1912, into land that formerly had belonged to the Hudson's Bay Company. Reclamation of this territory by the federal government would remove two-thirds of Quebec's landmass.

The most familiar position on the subject of the north is that the territorial transfers of 1898 and 1912 were made from the federal government to a Canadian province, and that one of the implicit conditions of the transfer was that the northern lands would remain part of Canada. Of course this thought was not expressed explicitly either in legislation or in public debate at the time the transfers took place. In those days, the idea of Quebec separating was unthinkable. Neither Sir Wilfrid Laurier, who presided over the 1898 transfer, nor Sir Robert Borden, who authorized the transfer of 1912, anticipated that Quebec would ever become an independent state. Therefore, it is a fair assumption that neither man intended his actions to be the basis for an eventual cession of territory to a foreign country.

The 'implicit condition of transfer' argument is so well known that it can be found almost anywhere. The version below is taken from a letter to *Saturday Night* magazine:

> When Quebec was defined in Confederation in 1867, it was as a British possession, and comprising a much smaller territory than it now administers. There is "Quebec," which is, more or less, territory within fifty miles of the St Lawrence River, and then there is a rather vast and relatively unoccupied hinterland to the north, which may be administered by Quebec but which, until the Statutes of 1898 (c.3) and the Quebec Boundaries Extension Acts of 1912, did not form part of the province.[33]

The most detailed discussion of the history of northern Quebec from a pro-partitionist standpoint is provided in Albert and Shaw's book. They demonstrate beyond any doubt that Quebec has no claim to its north predating the 1898 and 1912 cessions. They note that the lands along the east coast of Hudson Bay and James Bay were discovered by Henry Hudson in 1610 and claimed in the name of the king of England. These lands were granted in 1670 by King Charles II to his cousin, Prince Rupert, along with all other lands drained by rivers flowing into these bays and the Hudson straits. For the next 199 years, this territory would be the private preserve of the Hudson's Bay Company.

The Company built trading posts and forts along the coast of the bay, and conducted a profitable business there until the 1680s, when the Sieur d'Iberville captured the forts for France. In 1697, France won sovereignty over the territory under the terms of the Treaty of Ryswick, but by the terms of the Treaty of Utrecht in 1713, Rupert's Land was transferred back to Britain. "This time," Albert and Shaw write, the matter of sovereignty was "signed and sealed 'à perpetuité' as the Treaty of Utrecht stated."[34]

Shortly after Confederation, Rupert's Land was transferred from the Hudson's Bay Company to Canada in return for an indemnity of 300,000 pounds. Both the Albert-Shaw text and the Bercuson-Cooper book carefully note that this was not a transfer of sovereignty, which remained vested in the Imperial Crown. Rather, Canada was paying the Company for the improvements that had been made during the two centuries of its *administration* of the territory. The same procedure (minus the indemnity) was used for transferring the eastern parts of Rupert's Land to Quebec in 1898 and 1912. This leads Albert and Shaw to write:

> Sovereignty over Rupert's Land was given to Canada as a kind of dowry in order to strengthen the "marriage" of the provinces. If the Canadian "marriage" were ever dissolved, the territory of Rupert's Land, if it had to be taken away from Canada, would, if anything, logically revert to Great Britain, and not to the departing "son in law."[35]

David Varty gives this argument its fullest expression in *Who Gets Ungava?* He reviews the legislation by which Quebec's share of Rupert's Land was transferred from federal to provincial control. Varty refers to this region as "Ungava," which was its name when it was part of the Northwest Territories.

He finds that these lands were not awarded outright to Quebec, but were granted in trust for the Crown. Specifically, they were transferred from "the Crown in right of Canada" to "the Crown in right of Quebec." This means that in strict legal terms the Queen continues to exercise sovereignty over Ungava, and has only transferred trusteeship to Quebec. Should Quebec violate the conditions of its trusteeship by becoming an independent republic, it would forfeit its right of administration:

> The declaration of independence by the Republic of Quebec itself terminates the contractual relationship with its principal,

the Crown. Quebec's renunciation of its jurisdiction occurs by reason of Quebec's declaration that the laws and constitution which granted Quebec jurisdiction are no longer applicable to Quebec. . . . The beneficial use of Ungava would return to the Crown in right of Canada, with the underlying title remaining vested in the Crown.[36]

The Kingdom of Quebec

The argument for partition from Crown sovereignty suffers from a fatal flaw: it assumes that Quebec will separate from Canada as a *republic*. Should Quebec become an independent monarchy, and retain Queen Elizabeth as its head of state, the whole argument for reclaiming the north would fall apart. After meeting with David Varty shortly after the publication of his book in 1991, I wrote to him about this problem. His response was that Quebecers are too anti-monarchist to tolerate such a solution.

This reply is as flawed as his original argument; there is a great deal a country will do to retain two-thirds of its territory. Moreover, there is a tidy historical precedent for this sort of situation. After Ireland gained its independence in 1921 as the Irish Free State, it retained the monarchy for over twenty years. The Irish dislike for the Crown far exceeded any distaste expressed by the Québécois, but the Irish understood the political value of retaining the Crown—for a few decades at least.

There remains, in addition, the obscure question of whether sovereignty over Canadian territory is exercised by the Queen in her capacity as monarch of the United Kingdom or as Queen of Canada. If it is in the former capacity, then the precedent of transferring territory from one Crown possession to another while retaining British Crown sovereignty was clearly established by the cession of Rupert's Land to Canada in 1869. Quebec's lands would remain under the sovereignty of the British Crown both before and after the formation of a sovereign Quebec state. If sovereignty is exercised through the Canadian Crown, then the practice of transferring territory from the sovereign jurisdiction of one Crown to another has been established by the transfer of all Canada's territory from the British Crown to the Canadian Crown as Canada gradually gained its full legal independence between 1867 and 1982. A further transfer from the Crown of Canada to the Crown of an independent Quebec would constitute no breach of precedent.

In either case, the legal grounds for reclaiming the North on the basis of Crown sovereignty are not strong.

The Crown sovereignty argument suffers from yet a further flaw: it does not distinguish the North in any legally significant way from the St. Lawrence 'heartland' of French Canada, which was ceded by the French Crown to the British Crown by the Treaty of Paris in 1763. An additional ninety-three years of British sovereignty over the north (with a sixteen-year gap between 1697 and 1713) can hardly be expected to make the region a special case in any important sense.

The same Crown sovereignty that exists over the North makes it impossible for Quebec to legally secede from Canada and become an independent republic, but all serious commentators on Canadian politics, including the authors of each of the various partition plans, admit that this right will have to be granted if it is demanded by a majority of Quebecers. By using the Crown sovereignty argument in one instance while letting it pass in another, Varty and the others remove any real sense of consistency from what is already a weak legal case.

The Historical Claim to the South Shore of the St. Lawrence

Far more tenuous historical arguments, and ones which are likely to prove even more contentious than those in favour of repossessing the North, have been presented to justify the removal of other regions from Quebec. A particularly thorough historical argument for continued Canadian sovereignty over the south shore of the St. Lawrence River is presented in the Albert-Shaw proposal.

Albert and Shaw argue that an independent Quebec should be reduced to the historic boundaries of New France. They maintain that Quebec's independence would, in legal terms, cancel the cession of 1763. Canada, they stress, owns its territory by virtue of lawful inheritance from the British Empire, while Quebec owns its territory in one of two ways: some is traditional British territory (like Rupert's Land) held in trust by Quebec, while other areas are an inheritance from the old French Empire on the banks of the St. Lawrence. It follows that any Quebec territory which was not a part of New France at the time of the Conquest can be considered to be part of Quebec today only because Quebec is still a Canadian province. Should Quebec separate, this territory would legally revert to Canada, for the same reasons that Rupert's Land did.

Albert and Shaw interpret New France's boundaries as excluding not only Rupert's Land, but also the entire region lying south of the St. Lawrence River. They refer to this region as "The South Shore."

In making the claim that Rupert's Land was not part of New France at the time of the Conquest, they are on solid ground. However, their historical case for the ownership of the South Shore rests on some pretty extreme territorial claims. They base their arguments on the strident claims of Britain's 18th Century imperialists, who insisted that the northern boundaries of the king's New England and Nova Scotia colonies extended right up to the southern bank of the St. Lawrence River. This view came to be embodied in the official documents and correspondence of the British civil service in the years before the Treaty of Paris transferred sovereignty in 1763, much as Quebec's present-day claim to Labrador makes its way into all variety of maps published by the province.

To prove their point, Albert and Shaw cite an epistle penned by Lord Halifax to the Board of Trade shortly after the Conquest. Halifax declared that the new crown colony of Quebec would henceforth include not only the territory of New France, but also chunks of land that had formerly belonged to older colonies. Quebec would now, Halifax wrote, be delimited "as comprehending all such part of Canada on the north side of the River St. Lawrence, and all such parts of His Majesty's antient [ancient] colonies of Nova Scotia, New England, and New York on the South side of the said river as lie within the limits above mentioned. . . ."[37]

Of course, what Quebec's new boundaries really reflected was the fact that, now that they possessed the colony, the British had found it necessary to adjust their definition of its legal limits to reflect reality rather than their sated imperial aspirations. The Halifax letter is nothing more than an admission that the British legal claim to the territory in question had never been realistic and had in no way been a reflection of political or demographic reality.

Albert and Shaw continue on to admit that, before the Conquest, "Britain and France never did agree where, on the south side of the St. Lawrence River, the boundary was."[38] This does the authors credit as historians, but it does not strengthen their legal case, since France's most extreme claim would have given it possession of southern Ontario and much of the American Midwest. In fact, by

the historical criteria that Albert and Shaw have set forth, an
independent Quebec might not unreasonably lay claim to all of
Ontario east of Sault-Ste-Marie.

The grounds for extreme Québécois claims along these lines are
not strong, but that will not prevent them from being used as a foil.
Typical of the arguments that Canada can expect to face if it
seriously advances its historical claims is the following letter sent
by a Québécois reader to *Maclean's* in response to an article that had
presented the historical argument for partition:

> If certain Canadians believe that Canada could break away
> pieces of Quebec, then I suppose that the international courts
> could give Quebec back some of its original land, which in-
> cluded parts of Manitoba, Ontario, New Brunswick, Nova
> Scotia, New York and Vermont.[39]

There is something innately arbitrary about historical arguments of all sorts. They must pick and choose among past events,
emphasizing those which support their claims and disregarding or
rejecting as illegitimate those that do not. The latest historically-
founded claims to Quebec territory have been posed by the leaders
of militant factions at the Mohawk reserves of Kahnawake and
Kanesatake, who have indicated that their nation is the rightful
owner of Montreal, the Eastern Townships, and parts of Ontario,
Vermont, and northern New York. In the 'who got here first'
contest, the Natives are hands-down winners.

Not only are such legal and historical arguments usually factu-
ally weak; they are also politically irrelevant. After all, speaking
from the perspective of strict legality, Quebec cannot separate at all.
There is no provision in the Canadian constitution for the secession
of any part of the country. Yet Canadians have long understood the
reality that, unless we are willing to tolerate a civil war, Quebec
must be permitted to secede if the majority of its population so
chooses, regardless of the legal niceties involved.

Realistically, the same rule of respecting local majorities must
apply to each of the regions of Quebec. If any region of the province
wishes to be a part of an independent republic, this wish will have
to be respected if violence is to be avoided.

2. The National Security Argument

Just as much as demographic realities limit our ability to implement historically-based partition plans, they also militate against the argument presented by the advocates of the second line of thought on partition. This is the claim that if Canada is to survive as a united country, it must remain a contiguous whole. This would require the creation of an all-Canadian transit corridor between the four Atlantic provinces in the east and the five provinces to the west of Quebec. A corridor cannot be created, according to the advocates of this line of thought, unless most or all of the 'South Shore' of the St. Lawrence remains Canadian territory.

The Pakistanization of Canada?

Canada's situation is usually represented as being parallel to the situation of Pakistan during the period following that country's independence, when East Pakistan (now Bangladesh) and West Pakistan were separated by over 1,000 miles of Indian territory. In the end, so the argument goes, only a direct link between east and west will keep this country from falling apart as Pakistan eventually did.

This argument ignores the fact that East and West Pakistan had no cultural or linguistic bonds, and had been united by the departing British solely because they shared the same religion. It is a little difficult to believe that a road link between the two halves of Pakistan would have saved that unhappy union. As well, there are numerous historical instances of successful nations which have consisted of non-contiguous chunks of territory. The most obvious present-day example is the state of Alaska, which is in no danger of being lost to the United States despite its geographical isolation.

Creating Civil Strife in the Name of Civil Security

The Alaska analogy has been suggested by a number of prominent Canadians, including Newfoundland premier Clyde Wells. Still, it does not convince everyone. In a recent article in the Ottawa *Citizen*, Lionel Albert wrote that it is unreasonable to expect that Canada would be granted full and free rights of passage across Quebec soil, or even across American soil. To make his point, he cites an example:

> In the First World War, everything for our Canadian troops fighting in Flanders had to go through Maritime ports. Until the middle of 1917, when the U.S. entered the war, there was

only one route available, the Canadian National through Levis.
The Canadian Pacific line to Saint John, New Brunswick, via
Vermont and Maine, could not be used because the U.S. was
neutral and its laws forbid the carriage of foreign troops and
military supplies.[40]

Bercuson and Cooper discuss the issue in *Deconfederation*, and
are even more direct:

> The reason why the existence of a foreign state athwart the St.
> Lawrence would be unacceptable to Canada is obvious from a
> glance at a map. Territorial contiguity is, very simply, a vital
> Canadian national interest. . . . The experience of European
> nations regarding enclaves (or exclaves) of territory requiring
> passage through a foreign state indicates that a general, though
> not a universal, right of passage exists. Private and civilian
> government officials are normally allowed free access from the
> home state to the enclave to perform normal private and
> official tasks. Free access is usually denied when the home state
> seeks to send military forces into the enclave. It is clear that a
> sovereign Quebec capable of interdicting the movement of
> military equipment to Canadian Forces bases in Atlantic Can-
> ada would be unacceptable to Canada.[41]

This is a very peculiar argument. Bercuson and Cooper assume
that the normal practice between other nations is the only option
available to Canada and Quebec, and that nothing different can be
devised. This is nonsense. The Canadian government could—and
should—insist, as a non-negotiable condition of independence, on
the right of free road and rail passage along the Trans-Canada
highway and the main CNR and CPR lines, and free navigation along
the St. Lawrence Seaway. Every indication suggests that the newly
independent state of Quebec would grant them to us willingly.

Rights of Passage

This proposal is not so far from standard international practice
as Bercuson and Cooper seem to think. Military passage is denied
to three of the four presently existing enclaves in Europe (Belgian-
owned Baerle-Duc in the Netherlands, as well as the Italian enclave
of Campione d'Italia and German-owned Busingen, both of which
are surrounded by Swiss territory), but it is permitted in the case of
the fourth. Armed Spanish military personnel are permitted to

cross French soil to gain access to the Spanish enclave of Llivia. Another example: during the Second World War, Germany retained the right to use Switzerland's main north-south rail line, which passes through the St. Gotthard Pass, to transport supplies, including war materiel, to Italy. The Swiss tolerated this arrangement because it seemed better than the obvious alternative of Nazi occupation. The Germans tolerated it because it seemed preferable to attempting to occupy hostile territory at great expense. Not to put too fine a point on it, this is precisely why such an arrangement would work between Canada and Quebec.

A similar arrangement was worked out on a somewhat less sinister basis between the Allied Powers following the Second World War. The survival of West Berlin as a viable city was made possible by the possession by the West Germans of transit rights across East German territory into the city. A highway route, a rail line, and three air corridors remained open to the isolated city throughout the Cold War, although a brief attempt was made by the Soviets in 1949 to shut down this access. This blockade attempt resulted in the famous and hugely successful Berlin airlift.

As well, even Bercuson and Cooper admit that the government of Quebec could not cut off traffic of any sort between the Eastern and Western parts of Canada without suffering retaliation in kind. The Gulf of St. Lawrence, which represents Quebec's only access to the open sea, is a *mare closum*: it is entirely within Canada's territorial waters. If an independent Quebec were to try to cut or hinder communications between Canada's two constituent parts, Canada could just as easily sever Quebec's access to the rest of the world.

It seems far more likely that the leaders of an independent Quebec would be positively anxious to agree to terms which would protect the viability of Canada as a country and a trading partner, especially as concerns free transportation rights. As long ago as 1976, Quebec premier René Lévesque wrote:

> With this strange new-coloured Quebec on the map between Ontario and the Maritime provinces, Canada must be kept from feeling incurably "Pakistanized," so we must address ourselves without delay to the problem of keeping a land bridge open with as much free flow of people and goods as is humanly possible; as much and more as there is, I would imagine, between Alaska and the main body of the United States over the western land bridge.[42]

Jacques Brossard has gone further and stated that "without a doubt" Quebec would offer Canadians the right to pass across Quebec's territory along the Trans-Canada Highway and the CN and CP rail lines without being subject to taxes or other forms of government control.[43] In essence, this is an offer to create a sort of limited corridor along these routes.

Canada would probably not have to wait long for such a guarantee. This is because Quebec will have to grant extensive transit rights if it hopes to be admitted to the world economic community. In the present day it is impossible for a country to be a serious trade power if it is not a signatory to the General Agreement on Tariffs and Trade, or GATT. GATT is a multilateral treaty guaranteeing all signatory states most-favoured nation status in regard to tariff concessions. All important industrial nations are signatories. The Canada-U.S. Free Trade Agreement, in which the Parti Québécois desperately wants to make Quebec a partner, is technically an addendum to GATT.

GATT has a number of clauses regarding rights of transit through the territory of signatory states. Article 5 of the GATT treaty states:

> There shall be freedom of transit through the territory of each contracting party, via the routes most convenient for international transit, for traffic in transit to or from the territory of other contracting parties.[44]

The article also prevents unnecessary restrictions and delays upon traffic, and guarantees exemptions from transit charges, other than for services rendered, as well as from customs duties. Although these rules are primarily intended for trans-shipments of physical goods, in Canada's case they would apply to the transport of passenger traffic as well.

Finally, it should be noted that the separatists have always gone to great lengths to convince the rest of Canada that they would not interfere with the free operation of the St. Lawrence Seaway. Even if the separatists were not sincere, they would have little enough choice in the matter. The St. Lawrence Seaway is an international waterway by treaty with the United States and other countries. It is, in effect, a water-borne corridor, and is guaranteed to remain such in perpetuity. The Treaty of Washington, signed in 1871, makes this clear:

> The navigation of the St. Lawrence, ascending and descending

from the 45th parallel of north latitude, where it ceases to form
the boundary between the two countries, from, to, and into the
sea, shall forever remain free and open for the purpose of
commerce to the citizens of the United States, subject to any
laws and regulations of Great Britain or the Dominion of
Canada, not inconsistent with such privilege of free navigation.[45]

The transit rights of American ships were further strengthened
by an exchange of diplomatic notes in 1954, which provided that
Canada would consult the United States before enacting any regu-
lation affecting American shipping in the Canadian parts of the St.
Lawrence River.[46]

As the successor to Canadian sovereignty in the lower St. Lawrence, Quebec would also be successor to Canada's treaty rights
and obligations regarding the river (just as Canada inherited Great
Britain's treaty rights and obligations on the St. Lawrence as it
gained independence). Quebec would be legally unable to restrict
the rights of other nations to use the St. Lawrence by any other
means than bilateral negotiations with each of these nations. This
would be tough work, since over the years Ottawa has granted "most
favoured nation" status to many countries. Once such status has been
granted, Canada (and, therefore, Quebec) is legally obliged to grant to
the recipient nation all transit rights accorded to the Americans.

Oddly enough, Canada itself would not have "most favoured
nation" status in the Quebec-owned portions of the St. Lawrence
Seaway because it has never signed a treaty with itself. (This
situation would end as soon as Quebec signed the GATT Treaty.)
This suggests at first that a vindictive Quebec government could
place selective restrictions solely on Canadian vessels passing
through the St. Lawrence. However, a closer look shows that even
this action would be illegal. As successor to sovereignty to part of
the St. Lawrence Seaway, Quebec would automatically become a
partner in the International Joint Commission that regulates the
operations of the St. Lawrence. Canada, as sovereign over other
parts of the Seaway and an existing partner in the Commission, is
guaranteed the right to complete access to the entire length of the
Seaway. In return, ships registered in Quebec would be guaranteed
full access, through Canadian and American waters, to all parts in
the Great Lakes.

Much Ado About Nothing

In general, talk of the need for corridors seems to be the result of a serious misreading of the Québécois nationalist agenda. This misreading assumes that an independent Quebec would for some reason want to make life difficult for its neighbours. The impracticalities of this sort of isolationism are apparent to all parties in Quebec. Within the province, the major post-independence issues are seen as including entrance into the existing free trade deal between Canada and the United States, and the sale of more electricity to New England. This is not the agenda of an isolationist state.

The kind of ignorance that leads many otherwise normal people to support inflammatory corridor proposals is typified by a recent *Maclean's* column in which Peter C. Newman describes an interview with Winnipeg financier and grain merchant George Richardson, "The most powerful businessman west of the lakehead." Both Richardson and Newman reveal a total lack of awareness of the treaty obligations that require Quebec to keep the St. Lawrence Seaway open. Newman writes:

> I asked [Richardson] a practical question: if Quebec did separate, how would he get his grain to transatlantic markets? "It would have to be worked out," he replied noncommittally, then leaned forward and, in an unexpected aside, speculated: "We might have to go down the Mississippi."[47]

The fact that Canada does not need sovereignty over a transit corridor between Ontario and New Brunswick does not mean that there will not be a need for corridors elsewhere in Quebec. The value of corridors is that they permit unimpeded access to enclaves when the surrounding country is hostile to the existence of these enclaves. This was what made the air corridor to West Berlin so valuable when the Soviets blockaded the city in 1949.

It is possible that following partition, Canada would be left in possession of one or more enclaves within the territory of a sovereign Quebec. It is safe to assume that Quebec's leaders would be considerably less generous about granting access to such enclaves, which they would regard as illegitimately removed from the territory of their country, than they would be about transit rights between Ontario and New Brunswick. Perhaps they might even violate their GATT obligations and hinder traffic to and from the enclaves. It is in the context of such enclaves that the concept of corridors ought to be discussed.

Cross-Border Shopping, Klondike-Style

Further evidence that lack of direct access will not be a problem for Canada is indicated by a forgotten chapter in our own history. Canada has been cut off from a large chunk of its own territory once before in the past century. There was a time when Canada owned what was effectively an enclave within the territory of the United States. Before the construction of the Alaska Highway in the 1940s, the Yukon was reachable only by passing through Alaska. The two most popular routes during the Gold Rush of 1898 were by foot through the Chilkoot Pass, and by boat up the Yukon River. Both routes originated on American territory. The White Pass Railway, completed just as the Gold Rush ended, also originated in the United States.

It is true that the Yukon possesses a very long border with British Columbia, an even longer border with the Northwest Territories, and also a northern sea coast, but this was all unexplored territory at the time. When Dr. Kristian Falkenburg set out from Edmonton in September 1897 to chart an all-Canadian route to the Yukon, he took twenty-two months to reach his destination and almost died en route. He was lucky. According to popular historian Pierre Berton, of the 766 men, nine women and 4,000 horses who set out via this route, only 160 men made it to the Klondike, and every last pack animal died on the trail.[48]

Throughout the period that the Yukon was effectively an enclave, the United States was a far greater menace to Canadian sovereignty than Quebec can ever hope to be. America was in an expansionist mood at the time; the peak year of the Klondike gold rush was also the year that the United States occupied Cuba and the Philippines, and annexed Puerto Rico. During this period there was also an emotional boundary dispute along the Canada-Alaska border. The American president who brought the dispute to a conclusion in 1903 was Theodore Roosevelt, who openly advocated annexing not just the Yukon, but all of Canada.

Despite everything, Canada's sovereignty over the Yukon was never challenged, and Canada's right of egress over American territory was never questioned. The moral of the Yukon story is simply that between civilized neighbours, civilized behaviour will rule even in unconventional situations. This rule holds true of

Quebec as well, which has been more civilized than most places on Earth for most of its history.

In short, contact between east and west will not be a serious problem for Canada, and is not a valid justification for taking control of the South Shore.

Quebec as Security Risk?

As a further justification for the Canadian seizure of the South Shore, Bercuson and Cooper speculate that "an independent Quebec, at least one that possessed the same borders as the Province of Quebec, would certainly pose problems for Canadian and American strategic defence."[49]

They do not explain why this would be the case, although other authors have tried. In 1977, one particularly imaginative novelist produced a volume entitled *The Beachhead Principle*[50], which featured a cover illustration with a map of Quebec coloured ominously red, spreading forth grasping, tentacle-like arrows to engulf the rest of North America.

The idea of Quebec as a mainland Cuba was hard enough to take seriously fifteen years ago. Today, with the United States dominating the globe as no single power has done since the days of Napoleon, the thought of Quebec as a strategic menace is laughable. Moreover, it is difficult to follow Bercuson and Cooper's logic as they try to make a connection between this imagined threat and Québécois sovereignty over the South Shore. Surely a belligerent, truncated Quebec, shorn of the South Shore and half its population, would be more likely to fall into the hands of radicals and make dangerous alliances than would a Quebec that has retained most of its territory and the vast majority of its francophone population.

"Battle Not With Dragons, Lest Ye Become a Dragon . . . . "

The most obvious objection to the seizure of all or part of the South Shore is that it would create more problems than it would solve. This is the most thickly populated part of Quebec. Outside the Eastern Townships and the southern Gaspé, the South Shore is virtually 100 percent French. In the event of Quebec's separation, almost all these people would want to be part of the new country, not of Canada. To deny them this right would be to invite violence. No great skill is required to pull up railway tracks or to attack motorists with Ontario or New Brunswick license plates on isolated stretches of the Trans-Canada Highway. Use of this corridor, ostensibly so vital for the sake of Canadian troop movements, might be possible only if troops were stationed there permanently. Will Canada have to secure the South Shore with its own version of the Black-and-Tans?

All of this is unrealistic, and totally unnecessary, as even Bercuson and Cooper reluctantly admit. Having eloquently argued for the creation of a Canadian Ulster on the South Shore, they perform a complete *volte face* in the conclusion to their book:

> Since Quebec has no prior claim on the south shore of the St. Lawrence we assume that in the negotiations that would follow Quebec's declaration of independence Canada will secure that territory as part of its geographic boundaries. But even if we are wrong and Canadian negotiators give in to a misguided sense of charity, or to stupidity, or to cowardice (or a combination of all three), they will surely secure the right of free and innocent passage across Quebec in exchange for the right of Quebec ships and aircraft, military and civilian, to free and innocent passage through the St. Lawrence Seaway, the Strait of Belle Isle, and Cabot Strait. The example that is most frequently cited to prove how impossible it would be for the Atlantic provinces to remain part of Canada—the failure of Pakistan to survive in two parts—is not relevant. Quebec will be a friendly country sharing mutual interests.[51]

3. In Defence of Democracy

Historical arguments and the corridor/security argument form the first two lines of thought on partition. The third holds forth the democratic model used so successfully in Switzerland. This is partition on the basis of local majority vote, relying on the majority will of local residents to decide the country in which they wish their communities to remain.

SUMMARY

In surveying the extremist nature of most partition plans, it is apparent that their authors have not thought to pursue a purely democratic solution to the partitioning of Quebec and as a result have introduced the dangers of extreme Québécois reactions and of violence into the equation. From these plans we learn that:

- **Historical / legal arguments must not be used to justify land transfers.**
  The problem with historical and legal arguments is that they are highly subjective, and tend not to have any relation to the demographic realities of current times. On a historical basis, Quebec could lay claim to much of Canada and the United States, and Natives could lay claim to all of Quebec and the rest of Canada as well! These positions are laughably impractical, given current population patterns, but some promoters of Quebec partition seem intent on flying in the face of reality.

- **Canadians need not view an independent Quebec as a threat to Canadian national security.**
  The absence of land links between Ontario and New Brunswick does not justify territorial seizures. It would not be in Quebec's interest to hinder Canadians from crossing its territory. Moreover, Quebec would be limited by both international law and existing treaty obligations in its ability to limit transit rights.

Perhaps the most disturbing aspect of these unsophisticated partition plans is that:

- They are preoccupied with the erroneous idea that Canadian national security can be guaranteed through territorial unity.

- They advertise Quebec as some sort of menace that will seek to ruin Canada after leaving Confederation.

- They promote the idea of seizing land for road corridors to link eastern and western parts of Canada without thought to the impact this would have on the people who live in the corridors.

- They speak of dictating terms to Quebec, without realizing that force will only generate an opposing show of force.

These partition planners have conjured up an imaginary threat emanating from an independent Quebec, and, by doing so, they have submerged in their plans the very mistakes that were made in Ireland and Yugoslavia that Canadians must seek to avoid.

CHAPTER FOUR

Applying the Swiss Solution in Quebec

The Need for a Comprehensive Secession Law in Canada

If the lessons of history are well learned by Canadians, there is no reason why partition in Quebec could not take place as peacefully and democratically as it did in Appenzell and the Jura.

The most important measure the federal government could take towards ensuring this goal would be to adopt a Secession and Partition Law as soon as possible. This would do two things:

1. It Would Encourage a 'No' Vote

By revealing that there are genuine costs attached to independence, a well-drafted federal partition law would make the voters of Quebec think twice about voting 'Yes' to separation. This point was emphasized well by Toronto lawyer James Arnett, a participant in a 1990 symposium held by the C.D. Howe Institute, on the dangers of Quebec separation:

> We must deal realistically, not emotionally or antagonistically, to help Quebec see the enormous real costs of independence. I do not think that Quebecers are hearing about those costs. It is conceivable that we could influence the debate in Quebec if we start talking about the possibility that Quebec would not have the entire land mass. . . .[52]

2. It Would Set the Rules of the Game

By setting the rules of the game in advance, the Canadian government would be taking control of the referendum process now in motion in Quebec. If no action is taken by the federal government until after a 'Yes' vote in the referendum, the franco-phone majority in Quebec will feel, quite justifiably, that it has been deceived by a duplicitous federal government which at first tried to lure the province to remain in Canada with honeyed words and false promises, and then turned on it with petulance and vindic-tiveness when this had failed.

This feeling will be greatly compounded if the federal govern-ment then produces a partition proposal which involves the sei-zure of northern Quebec or the South Shore of the St. Lawrence, on the basis of historical or legalistic arguments. At this point, Canada would be inviting a very unfavourable image upon itself not only in Quebec, but also in the world community, as the advocate of half-baked schemes to eviscerate Quebec and overthrow the dem-ocratically-expressed will of its majority.

Within Quebec, extreme or anti-democratic measures on the part of English Canada would have the effect of taking the initiative away from the 'moderate' separatists, who consider peace and good order to be an important aspect of independence, and throw-ing it to the extremists. Democratic measures having failed, the extremists could argue, other means will be necessary to obtain independence. This is the very same rhetoric that Canadians have found so admirable when it is expressed by the brave separatists of Slovenia, Kurdistan, and the Baltics. How ironic to find ourselves opposing it at home!

THE LEGAL MECHANICS OF PARTITION

The Legitimacy of Separation

The existence of federal secession and partition legislation would also make it difficult for the separatists to attempt to come up with *de facto* secession legislation of their own. This is what Quebec's nationalists have been steadily doing ever since Premier Daniel Johnson wrote his book *Egalité ou Indépendence* in the 1960s. No-where is separation discussed in the Canadian Constitution. At-tempts to split the country probably qualify as treason under the letter of our existing body of law. We have come, however, to accept that separatist efforts are completely legitimate. By an unwritten convention established when Canada tolerated a referendum on separation in 1980, we accepted that separation was a valid objective.

Continued silence in English Canada as the Quebec government produces reports and commissions on the mechanics of separation ensures that if independence is ever achieved, it will be on Quebec's terms rather than Ottawa's. It is Quebec that is creating the laws that will govern the terms of separation. For instance, Bill 150, which was passed by Quebec's National Assembly in 1991, calls for independence to be declared one year to the day after a 'Yes' vote in a referendum on independence. It is beyond the legal competence of the provincial legislature to produce such a law, since this constitutes a unilateral amendment to the Constitution of Canada, yet the law has never been referred to the Supreme Court by the federal government.

If a future federal government attempts to introduce the subject of partition after the fact of a positive vote in a Quebec referendum on independence, it will have violated its own unwritten secession law, which dictates that, by convention, we have given the Quebec legislature exclusive license to legislate on the subject of separation. This will not be a simple technicality. Should the issue get sticky and matters be brought before the tribunes of international law, Canada might very well find itself judged to be in violation of its own unwritten law for having attempted to partition Quebec.

The extent to which even the most strident opponents of Quebec nationalism have been forced by Ottawa's passive attitude to conduct the partition debate on Quebec's terms is revealed by this passage in David Varty's book on the partition of northern Quebec: "Thus, it would be important for Canada to make its demand for the Ungava territory within the *presently scheduled one year period* between a referendum vote in Quebec and a declaration of independence."[53] A new federal law would end this unbecoming situation.

Jacques Parizeau on the Legality of Partition

Many voices have suggested that partition would be legally impossible. The usual argument, presented regularly by Jacques

Parizeau to anyone who will listen, is that as long as Quebec remains a Canadian province, its territorial integrity is constitutionally guaranteed by Section 3 of the *British North America Act* of 1871. This section reads as follows:

> The Parliament of Canada may from time to time, with the consent of the Legislature of any Province of the said Dominion, increase, diminish or otherwise alter the limits of such Province, upon such terms and conditions as may be agreed to by the said legislature, and may, with the like consent, make provisions respecting the effect and operation of any such increase or diminution or alteration of territory. . . .

Parizeau maintains that this protection will last until the moment of separation and that from the moment of separation onwards, Quebec's right to its present boundaries will be protected by international law. Parizeau is too politic to say it, but under international law, any infringement upon the territory of a sovereign state is an act of war.

This position, so simple, so logical, and so final, is a source of immense frustration to many advocates of partition.

David Varty on the Legality of Partition

The only significant attempts at a response to Parizeau's arguments have been provided by David Varty in *Who Gets Ungava?* and by David Bercuson and Barry Cooper in *Deconfederation*. Varty's argument has already been dealt with in Chapter Three. To repeat it briefly, this argument holds that Quebec would, in declaring itself an independent republic, automatically forfeit legal sovereignty over the northern two-thirds of its territory, which it gained from Canada through two transfers in 1898 and 1912. This would happen because in Canada, sovereignty rests not in the legislative branch of government, but in the Queen. Thus, in rejecting the Queen, Quebec would partition itself. As I indicated when discussing Varty's proposal in detail, the argument is fundamentally flawed, since Quebec can easily secede as a newly-formed constitutional monarchy.

Bercuson and Cooper on the Legality of Partition

The Bercuson-Cooper attempt at a legal formula for partition is at least as convoluted as Varty's and is so unconvincing that even its creators do not believe that it can be made to work.

The authors suggest that it would be constitutionally permissible to excise territory from Quebec without the approval of the province's government as long as the boundary changes do not affect Quebec's borders with the three other provinces upon which it touches (Newfoundland, New Brunswick, and Ontario). They base this assertion on the wording of Section 43(a) of the *Constitution Act* of 1982, which states that the consent of a province's legislature must be gained before making "any alteration to boundaries between provinces." Section 43(a) does not make reference to any other types of territorial changes, so Bercuson and Cooper maintain that the right to make such changes without the approval of a provincial legislature is implicit in the section. As they put it:

> If there was proposed an alteration not to the boundary between provinces but between one province and the United States, this amendment would, one assumes, be subject to the seven-fifty provisions of the [constitution's] general amending procedure. [The 'seven-fifty' amending formula permits changes to be made to the constitution if they are approved by seven provinces containing fifty percent of Canada's population.][54]

On this basis, Bercuson and Cooper argue, Canada could create new provinces out of Metro Toronto, British Columbia's Lower Mainland, or (more to the point) parts of Quebec, such as the Eastern Townships. They also conclude, however, that most of the really important territorial changes included in their own partition plan would be unconstitutional, because they involve lands lying on Quebec's borders with other provinces.

Having decided that the proposal will not work, Bercuson and Cooper immediately jump to the conclusion that no other legal alternative is possible, and announce their advocacy of an illegal partition of Quebec in violation of Canada's own constitution. They have no illusions about the consequences of this action. When a government violates its own constitution, it is, in essence, launching a coup d'état, or a revolution from above. Bercuson and Cooper refer to this event as "a revolutionary founding or re-founding of the regime," and choose not to discuss the long-term consequences for the continued rule of law in post-secession Canada.

Answering Parizeau: A Formula for Legal Partition

Curiously, almost all participants in the partition debate seem to have forgotten that Quebec cannot legally secede until an amendment to the federal constitution has been adopted, redefining Canada's boundaries as excluding all (or some) of Quebec's territory, and explicitly stating that Canada recognizes Quebec's provincial government as the sole legitimate sovereign over this territory. Parliament could define Quebec's boundaries as it chooses in this amendment. This provides a legal mechanism for partition. In its simplest form, such an amendment could read, "1. Notwithstanding anything else stated in the Constitution of Canada, Quebec shall cease to be a province on such and such a date; 2. The claims of the Canadian government to any sovereign authority over the territory presently included within the bounds of the province of Quebec shall cease on the aforesaid date."

As written above, the amendment would grant an independent Quebec sovereignty over all its present territory. But, of course, the amendment could include clauses limiting the territory that would be permitted to leave Canada. The amendment to the Bernese cantonal constitution permitting the Jura to secede included detailed arrangements for a partition. This should be the model for the Canadian constitutional amendment.

At the back of this book I have reproduced the Bernese amendment. The essence of the amendment was recognition of the right of the Jurassians to self-determination, coupled with the right of individual localities within the seceding territory to decide whether to remain part of Berne. A Canadian constitutional amendment modelled on the Bernese example would require the approval of seven provincial legislatures from provinces with at least half the country's population. This condition being met, Section 3 of the *British North America Act* of 1871 and Section 43(a) of the *Constitution Act* of 1982 could both be overridden, and Quebec could legally be partitioned.

Damage Control

It is incomprehensible from the point of view of the Canadian national interest that the federal government continues to refuse to seize hold of the issue which is more likely than any other to make Quebecers vote against separation. Unfortunately, it is completely rational from a short-term point of view for the Conservative federal government and the Liberal federal opposition to keep silent on the partition issue, since partition is opposed by virtually all francophone Quebecers and the Quebec vote is vital to either party if it hopes to win the next election—even if this election proves to be Canada's last as a united country.

Because it is unlikely that either a Liberal or a Conservative government will be willing to alienate Quebec voters by producing a legal framework for separation and partition, we must assume that a partition law will not be produced by the federal government until it has already lost the initiative, and Quebec has already held a referendum on separation.

For this reason, the emphasis in the remainder of this chapter will be on damage control measures. I will review the disruption tactics likely to be used if the federal government waits until after a 'Yes' vote in the referendum and then tries to introduce a partition based upon the principle of local self-determination. It can be assumed that the Quebec government will do all it can to obstruct the local referendum process or anything else that has the potential to lead to partition. The tactics which it is likely to adopt are perfectly predictable, since most of them were tried twenty years ago by the Rassemblement jurassien, or else have been tested by other secessionist movements in similar situations.

In the case of each tactic, the Canadian hand would be greatly strengthened and the hand of the separatists substantially weakened if the federal government would get its act together and pass a comprehensive secession and partition law in advance of a province-wide referendum in Quebec. Be this as it may, any of these tactics may be tried in the course of the partition crisis, and Canada must be prepared to deal with each of them.

PARTITION SPOILER TACTICS

A Boycott of Local Referenda

One tactic would be for the separatists to encourage a boycott of local referenda on the theory that if enough francophones refused to participate, the voting results would be too skewed to be meaningful and would have to be abandoned.

The possibility that this tactic might be used in Quebec was recently raised by Professor Guy Laforest of Laval University, who

made the following response when asked about the possibility of a
Canada-wide referendum co-ordinated by Ottawa:

> Quebec nationalists like myself see Quebec as being autono-
> mous, as having the right to self-determination. So the national
> referendum for us is a Quebec referendum. A referendum run
> by the federal government in Quebec is an illegitimate act, and
> I for one suggest it would bring massive civil disobedience.[55]

This tactic was recently employed by Croatian separatists in the
Krajina region of southern Croatia, discussed previously in Chapter One. The Krajina region is mostly ethnically Serbian, which
explains the lopsided results of the May 12, 1991 plebiscite on
uniting with Serbia. Only 73 percent of eligible voters turned out to
cast their ballots, but a full 99 percent of those who did vote
favoured union with Serbia. It appears that virtually every Serbian
voter in the region participated, while almost every Croat boycotted the vote. Almost the opposite result took place in the
Croatia-wide referendum held a few days later, in which the vast
majority of ethnic Croats voted to secede from Yugoslavia.

As the Krajina example shows, such boycotts are not particularly good at disrupting the actual proceedings of a local referendum when the local majority is heavily weighted in favour of the
ethnic group that desires partition. On the other hand, the respective boycotts of the Serb-sponsored and Croat-sponsored referenda were highly effective in polarizing the two ethnic groups and
convincing each side that the other's referendum was illegitimate.
This is precisely the kind of mind-set that Canadians must avoid at
all costs.

The effectiveness of these boycotts was enhanced by the fact that
polling was conducted (or at least attempted) even in areas where
there was little or no local support for the goals of the two referenda. Activists were able to convince non-participants that their
natural apathy was an act of protest, and tensions were heightened.

Probably the best way to get around this risk would be to adopt
a variation of the procedure which was used to initiate the local
referenda in the Jura region. The results of the Jura-wide referendum were considered binding upon all districts with the exception
of those in which at least one-fifth of the registered voters were
willing to sign a petition demanding a local referendum on
whether to remain in Berne. Only in these districts were referenda
permitted. When the district-wide votes had been taken, the same

rule requiring a petition signed by one-fifth of all registered voters applied to individual communes. This provision kept down the total number of local referenda and rendered an effective boycott impossible.

The Rassemblement jurassien, for all its dislike of local referenda, was faced with a simple choice: if it participated in the local referenda, it would be able to actively campaign in each community, encouraging individuals to vote in favour of remaining within the new canton. In doing so, it stood a chance of actually changing the outcome of some of the closer local votes. If it had insisted upon a boycott, it would have thrown the field open to the anti-separatists.

In the end, the pragmatic course of unwilling but active participation was chosen. I suspect that this is the option which the separatists in Quebec would also choose, if local referenda were only being held in regions where there was local interest.

Assuming that the Bernese system described above were used in Canada, consider the results of a boycott sponsored by the government in Quebec City. The separatist forces would be clearly distinguishing themselves as the enemies of local democracy and local self-determination. In place of these ideals they would only be able to present the unappealing ideology of self-determination for the French-speaking Québécois majority—but not for anybody else. Such a stand would likely alienate some voters who might otherwise be willing to vote in local referenda in favour of their community remaining in an independent Quebec.

While polls indicate that it is unlikely that many anglophones, Natives, or immigrants would vote under any circumstances to remain in an independent Quebec, the same cannot be said for the 291,000 Quebecers of mixed French and English, or mixed French and immigrant origins.[56] These individuals live disproportionately in communities which have ethnically mixed populations and are likely to be affected by a few swing votes. Also over-represented in these swing areas are people who have entered into mixed French-English marriages, and are presumably willing to consider life in Canada or in an independent Quebec. The Quebec government could not afford to alienate either of these groups of voters. All of this militates towards the local referendum process being tacitly accepted by the Quebec government, even as it publicly condemns the whole process as illegitimate.

When the realistic choices are narrowed to either a series of boycotted local referenda that result in a partitioned Quebec which retains only 75 percent of its population, or active participation in local referenda that result in a partitioned Quebec which retains 85 or 90 percent of its population, the separatists will almost certainly choose the second option.

What if Quebec Declared Independence Unilaterally?

A frequently discussed disruption tactic that might be used to pre-empt local referenda is a unilateral declaration of independence, sometimes referred to as 'UDI.' Following UDI, all Canadian law, including any local-referendum legislation, could be declared null by the new national Quebec government, and individual Quebecers could be denied the right to participate in or administer local referenda.

This tactic would alienate moderates and advocates of democracy, besides being legally meaningless under Canadian constitutional law. But of course any government engaging in a unilateral declaration of independence would be attempting to place itself in a position where such considerations as moderate opinion and Canadian law would no longer have any practical significance.

Because Quebec's declaration of independence would have no meaning under Canadian law, the federal government would have the option of flatly refusing to recognize a unilateral declaration of independence until local referenda had been conducted. This would thrust the Quebec government back into the situation of either permitting the referenda to go ahead or of initiating force to suppress them. A provincial government desperate enough to try a unilateral declaration of independence might well attempt the latter alternative. All things considered, a simple refusal to recognize a unilateral declaration of independence is the crudest and least effective of the options open to Canada.

The Virginia Gambit

A more sophisticated but not much better alternative would be for a federal government faced with a unilateral declaration of independence to threaten to retaliate with a version of the formula used by the Lincoln administration in 1861 to partition the state of Virginia, which had then just seceded and joined the Confederacy.

Most of the mountainous western part of Virginia had fallen

under federal military control in the earliest stages of the Civil War. The inhabitants of the mountains were mostly poverty-stricken farmers who had little in common with the slave-owning lowlanders from the east who controlled the state government. This was sufficient reason, in the eyes of the federal government, to effect a partition of Virginia.

A bogus sitting of the Virginia state legislature was called in the town of Wheeling. Since this town was in Union hands, the legislators of the Confederate state of Virginia could hardly have been expected to attend. Only the pro-partition, pro-Union legislators from the west of the state arrived, and they voted overwhelmingly in favour of the creation of a new state. This vote was regarded as being sufficient to fulfil the constitutional requirement that state boundaries be altered only with the consent of the legislature. The real state legislature rejected the partition, of course, but by joining the Confederacy, it had rendered itself non-existent under United States law.

This at least was the interpretation of the Lincoln administration. West Virginia's tenuous legal existence has never been challenged. (To ensure that it never *would* be challenged, Virginia's acceptance of its reduced borders was made a condition of the state's readmission to the Union in 1870.)

Effected at a time of civil war, the West Virginia partition was not calculated to create goodwill, which suggests that it is not a very promising example. Still, in the event of a UDI, a Quebec version of the Wheeling convention could be called in the hope of attracting those members of Quebec's National Assembly for constituencies with non-francophone majorities. The Wheeling-style assembly could then vote to redefine the boundaries of the province to exclude all regions with non-francophone majorities. These areas would then be free to petition Parliament for admission to Canada as one or more provinces or territories.

Alternatively, the assembly could vote to redefine the *province* of Quebec as including only these same non-francophone regions, while recognizing the *independent state* of Quebec as including all the other parts of the present-day province. This would produce a province of widely dispersed enclaves and presumably would be only a temporary arrangement, to be followed by local referenda in each enclave on whether to join another province or seek some form of other status within Confederation.

There is no question that a West Virginia-style partition would be rejected by francophone Quebec as illegitimate. In addition, there is a good chance that the Supreme Court might judge the decisions of such an assembly to be meaningless. The real National Assembly would continue to operate in Quebec City throughout, and would probably have a thing or two to say about its rival. In short, this course of action would amount to partition by fiat with an admixture of legalistic make-believe. It would succeed only in making its sponsors look like cheap charlatans.

Honouring the Idea of a Unilateral Declaration of Independence

The best Canadian response to a unilateral declaration of independence would be for the federal government to take two parallel actions. Parliament should take immediate steps to amend the relevent sections of the Constitution to make Quebec's action legal, and to offer de facto recognition of Quebec's independence until the necessary changes to the Constitution had been made. This would show a respect for the right of self-determination at least as generous as the recent Soviet model, and a great deal more intelligent than the Yugoslav example.

The second action would be to unilaterally limit the geographical area of the independent state of Quebec to those parts of the province in which local majorities had voted in favour of separation. Canada would be in effect responding to a unilateral declaration of independence with a unilateral partition.

To make this work, Canada would have to be willing to immediately recognize the sovereignty of an independent Quebec over those parts of the province that had voted to secede, and to express a willingness to transfer sovereignty over any other locality in which over half the electorate would be willing to vote to join Quebec in a local referendum. The rest of the province would remain part of Canada.

This tactic would accomplish several things at once. First, by recognizing the Quebec government's right of complete sovereignty over all areas which had voted for separation in a province-wide referendum, it would show that Canada was sincere about its long-standing acceptance of the Québécois right of self-determination. Second, by giving the right to reverse their own decisions only to areas of the province that had voted initially against independence, the Canadian government would be subtly changing the terms of debate. Any further shifts of territory would be in

Quebec's favour. The separatists would now have nothing to lose and everything to gain from free local votes.

This does not mean that the Canadian government would be going soft. The strength behind the arrangement would be the enforcement of some relatively ungenerous temporary border arrangements. The frontier of the independent state of Quebec would no longer be the present provincial borders, but only those areas of the province that had voted 'Yes' in the provincial referendum on separation. Canada would have to show a willingness to unilaterally refuse to surrender sovereignty over these areas until local votes had been held.

One-Way Territorial Transfers in Northern Ireland

This distinction is important, as the example of the attempted partition of Northern Ireland shows. When the recommendations of the Irish Boundary Commission were leaked to the press in the autumn of 1925, the popular reaction in the Irish Free State was one of horror at the idea that even a small amount of the Free State's territory could be surrendered to Northern Ireland. This reaction was illogical since by the Commission's recommendations the Free State was to gain over five times the acreage and nine times as many Catholic citizens as it would be surrendering to the North. All things considered, the citizens of the Free State should have been congratulating themselves on an excellent bargain. Instead, the nationalists were so loath to consider shifting even a small part of the boundary southwards that they worked themselves into a fine frenzy and killed the partition deal. What seems to have happened is that somehow, between 1921 and 1925, the perfectly arbitrary borderline between the two Irelands acquired a life of its own, simply because it was there.

One-Way Territorial Transfers in the Jura

The same phenomenon took place in the wake of the Jura partition of 1979. Due to a flaw in the Bernese constitutional amendments governing secession and partition, two communes were left on the wrong side of the new border, and it has proved impossible to trade them back to where they belong. The amendments to the Berne constitution governing the local referenda included a clause designed to prevent the creation of enclaves. Only communes bordering the provisional frontier between Berne

and Jura or touching upon the territory of another Swiss canton
had been granted the legal right to decide their own futures.

One unexpected result of this anti-enclave clause was that two
very small communes, called Ederswiler (a German-majority commune on the Jura side of the new border) and Vellerat (a French-
majority commune on the Berne side of the frontier) were refused
the right to hold referenda determining the canton to which they
would belong, because they had not shared a border with any other
canton at the time the local referenda were held. Following the local
referenda, several neighbouring communes had switched cantons,
with the result that both Vellerat and Ederswiler now shared a
border with the canton to which their populations wished to
adhere. Under the terms of the referendum legislation, however,
there was no provision for further border adjustments on the basis
of territorial contiguity with a neighbouring canton. Thus the end
result was both undemocratic and unnecessary, since the cession of
the two communes from one canton to the other would have
created no enclaves.

The status of the two communes has continued to generate
heated controversy over the decade since separation. The Bernese
have expressed a willingness to part with Vellerat if the Jura will
transfer sovereignty over Ederswiler, but the Jurassian authorities
have insisted upon a one-way transfer of Vellerat without compensation. This is an unreasonable position, but not quite as unreasonable
as it first appears: Vellerat has a much smaller population than
Ederswiler, and its population is nearly unanimous in its desire to join
the Jura, while only a bare majority of the voters of Ederswiler cast
ballots against separation in the Jura-wide referendum of May 1974.
Thus, a trade would take a larger number of willing Jurassian citizens
out of the canton than it would place within the canton. Naturally the
Bernese do not see things this way, so the dispute continues.

The same kind of intransigence is also likely to be observed in
Quebec if the new country is asked to surrender or trade territory
after it has already declared independence.

One-Way Territorial Transfers in Quebec

Under the system proposed in this chapter, all territorial transfers occurring as a result of local referenda following a unilateral
declaration of independence would be to the benefit of the
Québécois state. No territory would be transferred back to Canada.

Because of the strongly anti-separatist bloc voting patterns in Quebec's various non-francophone communities, virtually every anti-separatist would have already cast his or her ballot for the 'No' side in the province-wide referendum before separation had taken place. The only vote-switching likely to occur in the second round of balloting would be francophone moderates who had voted 'No' in the first round but who would put their loyalty to Quebec ahead of their loyalty to Canada when finally forced to choose sides. Of course, there might be a limited number of French speakers who would in the final test put their loyalty to Canada before their loyalty to Quebec. These persons would have voted against separation in the first round of balloting, and therefore would almost certainly not represent a swing vote in any polls which had voted in the first round to go to Quebec.

Under this system, Canada would not be giving up any territory to which it has a justifiable democratic claim. It would have staged the second round of voting in such a way that the government of Quebec could not help but profit from the free and fair exercise of the right of local self-determination in a second round of voting.

If the federal government were to publicly adopt this partition plan in the period following a successful 'Yes' vote in a province-wide referendum on separation, it would become clear that neither a unilateral declaration of independence nor a voting boycott would then be to the advantage of the separatists. As a result, neither a boycott nor a unilateral declaration of independence would likely take place.

The obvious danger, of course, is that Quebec might, in blind disregard to all good sense, plunge ahead with a unilateral declaration of independence, and follow this up by responding with violence to an attempted unilateral partition. Violence is always the chief danger to be avoided under any partition arrangement, including the one I advocate, so the obvious question to be asked at this point is, under the democratic partition/*de facto* recognition system proposed here, would violence or terrorism serve the interests of the new Quebec state? If not, then it would be unlikely to occur.

One important factor militating against the use of violence is the fact that the advocacy by the Quebec government of undemocratic measures or of violence would have the effect of alienating persons in swing areas, causing them to throw in their lot with Canada.

In addition, I see no evidence that the Québécois have any

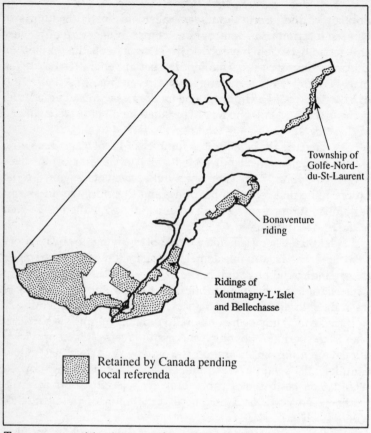

Township of
Golfe-Nord-
du-St-Laurent

Bonaventure
riding

Ridings of
Montmagny-L'Islet
and Bellechasse

Retained by Canada pending
local referenda

Temporary partition in event of UDI. (Fig. 10)

overwhelming desire to impose their will by force on unwilling minorities. The whole question of military action initiated by Quebec to stop the secession of its minority regions reminds me of a well-known episode in which René Lévesque was asked if he would use force to lead Quebec out of Confederation. That's not the issue, Lévesque is said to have responded; the real question is, if Quebec chooses to leave, will Canada use force to make us stay? The answer, as Lévesque knew, was that warmongering and imperialism are not part of the Canadian character.

Nor are they part of the Québécois character. Organized military opposition to a generous and democratic partition (and a partition that promises to become even more generous if only the Quebec government will participate in making the local referenda go its way) is, to my mind, inconceivable.

A final note should be made on the subject of unilateral independence and unilateral partition. I have developed a map of the probable borders of an independent Quebec in the interim period following a unilateral declaration of independence, in the brief period—perhaps six months—before local referenda could be conducted.[57]

According to my calculations, the temporary boundaries of an independent Quebec under this scenario would include the vast majority of southern Quebec's present landmass and most of its French-speaking population. This means that Quebec could begin functioning as a workable country immediately. It also means that the federal government would not be overextending itself by trying to control large areas in the interim period leading up to the local referenda, and that relatively few 'Yes' voters would be left, even temporarily, within the borders of Canada. Under these circumstances, the provocation to Quebec would be minimal, and I have no doubt that the Québécois would respond to the temporary situation with admirable political maturity.

A Call For Local Referenda In Other Provinces

A particularly effective disruption tactic would be for the separatists to demand, as a condition of accepting the validity of local referenda within Quebec, that the francophone areas in eastern Ontario and northern New Brunswick be given the opportunity to vote on seceding from Canada and joining Quebec. The idea here would be that English Canada would refuse to part with these areas, and that in so doing, it would reveal itself to be hypocritical. Partition, the separatists would then be able to observe, is intended as a tool against Quebec only. They would also have a strong argument that it be opposed by any means possible.

The idea of reciprocal referenda in anglophone Quebec and in francophone Ontario and New Brunswick was first broached by Parti Québécois ideologist Jacques Brossard as far back as 1976. Brossard may have felt that he had stumbled across a way to prevent a Jura-style partition of Quebec, since he made his suggestion while discussing the Jura model.[58] More recently, former Saskatchewan premier Allan Blakeney has made an almost identical proposal.[59]

Whatever the intellectual source, the idea of reciprocal local referenda is a perfectly just proposal from a democratic point of view, although the provincial governments in Ontario and New Brunswick would probably not see it this way.

My own inclination would be to permit or even encourage the holding of such referenda, should the separatists demand them. I suspect that Professor Brossard might be very disappointed with the results. The fellow-feelings of francophones residing outside Quebec with the Québécois elite are not particularly strong. The Franco-Ontarians and other non-Québécois francophones feel with some justification that they have been cast to the wolves by the government in Quebec City, which has over the past decade abandoned its traditional role of attempting to represent French speakers across the country. In 1988, for example, Quebec premier Robert Bourassa refused to criticize the premiers of Saskatchewan and Alberta when they passed legislation restricting francophone rights in those provinces. In return, the Alberta and Saskatchewan premiers remained silent when Bourassa crushed minority rights in Quebec a few months later with his restrictive language law, Bill 178. This was a cozy arrangement, but not one likely to make the francophone minorities in the other provinces feel that they can turn to the government of Quebec in moments of need.

What's more, the language rights of the Acadian minority in New Brunswick are protected by the province's bilingual status, which is entrenched in Sections 16 through 20 of the Canadian Charter of Rights and Freedoms. Unlike the sections of the Charter that Bourassa violated when he passed Bill 178, Sections 16 through 20 may not be overridden by the Charter's 'notwithstanding clause.' Even in Ontario, francophone rights are surprisingly well protected by provincial legislation—much more so than anglophone rights in Quebec.

Given these facts, I would not be surprised to see such a lack of pro-separatist enthusiasm among the francophones *hors Québec* that the separatists would be seriously embarrassed.

Even if I am wrong about this, the potential risks for Canada of holding referenda outside Quebec are minimal. Francophones form the majority in only one county in Ontario and four counties in New Brunswick. In some of these counties, anglophones form nearly half the population. This means that for any meaningful loss of territory to take place, nearly 100 percent of all French-speakers outside Quebec would have to favour joining Quebec.

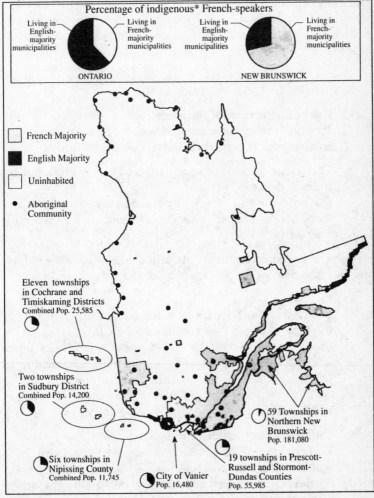

*Does not include the "immigrant" French-speaking population of overwhelmingly English-speaking cities like Toronto or Fredericton. The French-speaking populations of the English-majority cities of Ottawa and Moncton are included.

Population distribution of francophone Canada. (Fig. 11)

Moreover, these rural regions are far less populous and far less economically valuable than the industrial and financial centres of west-end Montreal. At the same time, if Canada permitted referenda to be held in border regions of Ontario and New Brunswick, the separatists would lose the moral high ground to the federalist side, and would find it difficult to gain support for further obstructionist measures.

SUMMARY

A comprehensive secession and partition law prepared and entrenched in the federal constitution would:

- **Establish the rules of the game.**
  Partition cannot be attempted without a pre-existing legal framework. A comprehensive law would do this.

- **Encourage a 'No' vote in any future Quebec referenda on independence.**
  Quebecers would see in advance the cost of partition and many would choose to remain in Canada as a preferable alternative.

Opponents of referenda may attempt one or more of the following tactics to disrupt the process of holding local referenda:

- **Boycotts.**
  To avoid voting boycotts that will damage the credibility of the local referenda on whether to remain in Canada, we should ensure that local referenda are only held in localities where at least 20 percent of the local population is willing to petition for a local referendum. Furthermore, the use of small voting areas (i.e. polls) as the base units of partition will ensure better turnout and representation.

- **Unilateral Declaration of Independence.**
  While a UDI would not be valid under Canadian law, it would be in the best interest of Canada to recognize Quebec's sovereignty over those areas of the province in which the majority had voted 'Yes.' The onus would be on Canada to maintain physical control over all other areas of the province and to insist that local referenda on partition be held in those areas that request it.

- **A call for referenda in other French areas in other provinces on whether to join Quebec.**
  From a Québécois nationalist point of view, partition is a one-way street. If English Canada were to respond positively to nationalist demands for local referenda outside of Quebec, the nationalist focus would change from trying to stop partition to trying to make it work their way. The actual risks to Canada of loss of population and territory would be minimal.

CHAPTER FIVE

Choosing the Units of Partition

The first step in establishing a partition procedure would be to choose the units within which to hold local referenda. In the Jura, this choice was easy. The region contained only two types of internal political divisions (seven districts and 134 communes). Referenda were held first in the larger divisions and then in the smaller ones.

In this country, the task is made difficult by the fact that geographically, Quebec is more complex than either Appenzell or the Jura. Before the creation of a separate Jura canton, the Jura region was divided into 134 communes, or municipalities, which were all of exactly equal legal standing. At the time of the 1974 referenda, they ranged in population from twenty-nine to 11,797.[60] In Switzerland, communal boundaries are not readily changed; most of the communes had frontiers that had been delimited before the Jura region joined Switzerland at the end of the Napoleonic wars. This made the communes the obvious choice as the units within which to conduct local referenda.

By contrast, Quebec contains an astonishing variety of local political divisions of varying levels of legal status. In 1988 Quebec contained 1,478 towns and cities, and 118 parcels of unorganized territory. In addition, it was home to thirty-eight Native reserves, twenty-two officially recognized non-reserve Native and Inuit settlements, and enormous stretches of provincially-owned land on which the Natives have retained semi-proprietary hunting and fishing rights.[61] As well, municipal boundaries are perpetually shifting in Quebec, and new towns are constantly being created, while others are being merged.

The choice of units is not restricted only to municipalities. Local referenda could be held on the basis of counties, electoral districts, or polls. Each of these systems will be examined in turn, always bearing in mind the principle that the desired result of the local referendum procedure is to permit as many individuals as possible to live in the country of their choice.

CONSIDERING THE UNITS OF DIVISION

As a rule, the larger the territorial divisions which are used for conducting local referenda, the greater the advantage to the separatists, and the cruder and less satisfactory the results in terms of actually representing local opinion.

Partition by County

From this perspective, a county-by-county partition would be the worst of all possible worlds. Quebec is divided into seventy-three counties, including the nearly empty northern half of the province, which is organized into a sort of super-county called *Le Territoire du Nouveau-Québec*.

The obvious advantage to the separatists of a partition on the basis of individual counties is that it would allow them to secede with their territory virtually intact, since only one of the province's counties (Pontiac County, just west of Ottawa-Hull) has a non-francophone majority. Only 11,000 anglophones, who form about one percent of Quebec's total non-francophone population, live in Pontiac County. Worse yet, awarding Pontiac County to Canada would inconvenience nearly as many people as it would help, since the county's population is 45 percent francophone.

To use counties as the primary tool for staging a local referenda on partition would therefore counteract the very criterion of true representation that is the whole justification for holding local referenda.

Partition by Municipality

A referendum conducted on a municipality-by-municipality basis

would be the closest analogy to the system used in the partition of the
Jura. Unfortunately, this is not in itself a recommendation. The municipally-based referenda in the Jura were successful in partitioning the
region by preference because they were conducted in municipalities
which were very small. The description in Chapter Two of the rioting
and violence that surrounded the referendum held in the town of
Moutier serves as a warning of what can happen in a civilized place
like Switzerland when the town is large and the vote is close. Leaving
aside the violence, the fact remains that in Moutier's local referendum
of September 7, 1975, 2,540 voters were able to impose their will on
a minority of 2,151 voters. The Moutier referendum was democratic, but not as democratic as it could have been.

The situation would be just as problematic, on a much larger
scale, in Quebec. To be sure, non-urban municipalities in Quebec
are small and usually fairly homogeneous. But in large, ethnically
mixed municipalities, minority votes which are huge in absolute
numbers could be overwhelmed by even larger majority votes.

Imagine that the vote in the City of Montreal was split precisely
on linguistic lines, with all the francophones supporting adherence
to Quebec and all the non-francophones in favour of continued
loyalty to Canada. In a straight vote, the city would go to Quebec,
and an unwilling non-francophone population of 293,000 would be
denied the right to live in the country of its choice. Assuming that
the rest of the province was partitioned on the basis of majority vote
in each municipality, a total of 850,000 non-francophones (78 percent of Quebec's entire non-francophone population), as well as
102,000 francophones would find themselves residing on the
wrong side of the new Quebec-Canada border.

In other words, to make municipally-based referenda work
properly, the municipalities would have to be subdivided for more
local vote-taking into some sort of smaller divisions such as
neighbourhoods, the wards in which city councillors are elected, or
perhaps census sub-districts. Any of these subdivisions would be
arbitrary. Their legitimacy would be attacked by those who are
eager to disrupt the partition process.

Municipalities and the Problem of Enclaves

A further difficulty of municipally-based referenda is that many
townships in which non-francophones form the majority are completely surrounded by other municipalities with francophone

majorities. The situation is most extreme in the north. At 119,197 square miles, the township of Baie-James is probably the largest municipality in the world. It completely surrounds numerous small towns and Indian reserves. The total population of these enclaves far exceeds that of Baie-James itself, and it is the Natives living on these reserves who make the most active use of Baie-James' vast wilderness stretches.

A municipally-based partition would leave Canada with eight enclaves and exclaves within the municipal boundaries of Baie-James. (An exclave is a piece of territory separated from its mother country but not surrounded by the territory of another country. In the case of the exclaves on the coast of Baie-James township, there would be direct water access to the rest of Canada.) There would be an additional four enclaves in the Ottawa River Valley, six in the Gaspé, eight in the Eastern Townships, and four on and around the Island of Montreal. Quebec would own one exclave, and two enclaves (including an enclave within one of the Canadian enclaves in the Eastern Townships).

Enclaves do exist elsewhere in the world and are usually perfectly functional, as I will explain in Chapter Six. A total of thirty enclaves, however, might be a bit much for any country to handle. Moreover, some of these enclaves are almost half French. For instance, the township of St-Georges-de-Clarenceville in the Eastern Townships has an anglophone majority of one, according to figures from the 1986 census. The existence of this enclave and a few others like it would presumably be very tenuous.

Partition by Electoral Districts

There are networks of federal and provincial electoral districts covering the entire territory of Quebec. The province contains seventy-five federal ridings, each of which elects one member to the House of Commons. Quebec is also divided into 125 provincial ridings (*circonscriptions electorales*), each of which sends one member to the National Assembly in Quebec City. The official results of the 1980 referendum were isolated and tabulated by provincial riding, and this is also probably how the results of any future province-wide referendum will be tabulated. This makes provincial electoral districts a logical alternative to municipalities as a basis for local referenda.

In strictly geographical terms, a partition on the basis of provincial

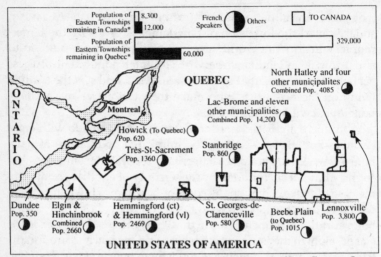

*Not including population of enclaves surrounded by Quebec territory. Population base: counties of Brome, Chateauguay, Compton, Megantic, Missisquoi, Richmond, Sherbrooke, St-Jean, Stanstead

Eastern Townships partitioned by municipality. (Fig. 12)

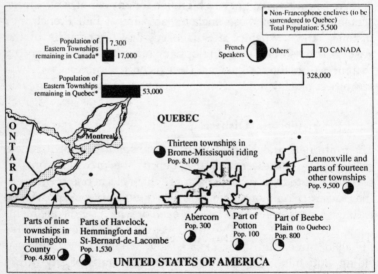

*Not including population of enclaves. Population base: counties of Brome, Chateauguay, Compton, Megantic, Missisquoi, Richmond, Sherbrooke, St-Jean, Stanstead

Eastern Townships partitioned by poll. (Fig. 13)

ridings would be a marked improvement over one based on municipalities. There are eleven ridings in which non-francophones form the majority of the local population. All of these ridings are contiguous, so Canada would not be left with a string of widely scattered enclaves. One disadvantage of this system is that all of the ridings are located on the western half of Montreal Island. The Cree and Inuit of the north, the English-speaking farmers of Pontiac County and the Eastern Townships, and the anglophone fishermen of the Gaspé and the Gulf North Shore would find themselves left out of Canada under this arrangement.

There is also the problem of the large population of each of these electoral districts. The population of the average riding in the province is 52,000. This means that the town of Moutier, which suffered riots during the Jura partition because of its large size, would fit into each riding six times over. Three of the ridings on the West Island have francophone minorities of over 45 percent. A bit further east, the riding of St-Louis has a non-francophone minority of 49.7 percent. All of this suggests that the kind of violence and intimidation which took place in Moutier in 1975 might well take place in western Montreal, on a much larger scale.

Another problem: once the Quebec government understands that a partition on the basis of ridings is to take place, the temptation to gerrymander the ridings in its own favour could prove overwhelming. Minimal changes to the boundaries of the ridings of Laurier, St-Laurent, Marguerite-Bourgeoys, or Nelligan would result in these four ridings losing their non-francophone majorities.

Even if this sort of practice does not take place, a partition formula which denies 198,000 francophones the right to remain in Quebec and forces 724,000 non-francophones to abandon their Canadian citizenship can hardly be called just, even if it is a marginal improvement on the county-based and municipality-based systems. Only 34 percent of Quebec's non-francophone population would be able to continue living in Canada under this system.

The Logical Choice: Partition by Polls

The obvious alternative is to look for a formula based upon smaller sub-units of the province's ridings. Every riding is divided into polls (*sections de vote*), each of which contains about 400 inhabitants, 250 voters and a single polling station, which is usually located in a firehall, school gymnasium, or other public building. Polls in

urban areas normally occupy a few city blocks, although they can
be small enough to contain a single apartment building. In rural
areas, polls can cover many square miles and hundreds of farmsteads, although they might never cross the boundaries of a municipality. The smallest rural townships share common boundary
lines with individual polls.

The idea of using polls as the basis for a partition is not new. It
was first suggested by no less an authority than the inimitable
Professor Jacques Brossard, who wrote in *L'accession à la
souveraineté et le cas du Québec*:

> We note here that it will be perfectly possible to know the
> "local" results [of a referendum on separation], because the
> votes must be calculated by "polls" or by ridings. . . . The
> political question to resolve in advance will be of knowing if
> one ought to take local differences into account or not. . . . [62]

Small Is Beautiful—And Just

The small size of polls makes them ideal from the point of view of
permitting the greatest number of people to live in the country of
their choice. Small areas have small minorities, and tend to be
pretty homogeneous. In a partition conducted by riding, very
homogeneous non-francophone polls would be swamped by the
larger francophone population of the riding in which they are
located. In a partition conducted by municipality, homogeneous
non-francophone neighbourhoods would be overwhelmed by the
vastness of cities like Montreal or Laval. Neither problem occurs
when the voting is conducted on a poll-by-poll basis.

"What If . . . ": Pontiac County Partitioned by Riding
and by Poll

To show why this is the case, consider the results of two imaginary
local referenda conducted in the riding of Pontiac County. This
riding, just west of Ottawa-Hull, overlaps the borders of Pontiac
County, but also includes the French-majority city of Aylmer in
neighbouring Gatineau County. The weight of this addition is just
enough to give the riding as a whole a bare French majority.
Assume that voting is divided with surgical precision on ethnic
lines, with all francophones supporting adherence to the new

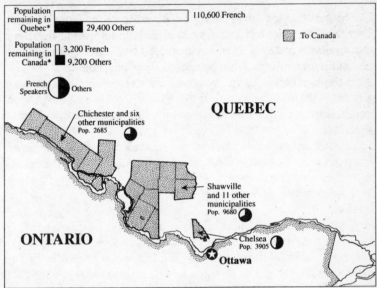

*Excluding the enclave of Chelsea which is completely surrounded by Quebec territory. Population base: ridings of Gatineau, Hull and Pontiac.

West Quebec partitioned by municipality. (Fig. 14)

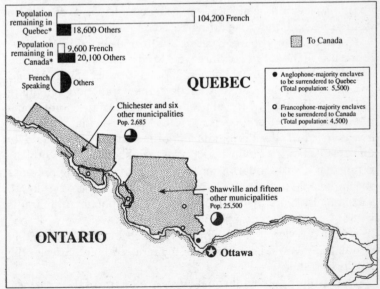

*Excluding Canadian enclaves completely surrounded by Quebec territory, and Quebec enclaves entirely surrounded by Canadian territory. Population base: ridings of Gatineau, Hull and Pontiac

West Quebec partitioned by poll. (Fig. 15)

Québécois state and all others voting to remain in Canada. This is not
very far from what history suggests is likely to happen in the event
that Quebec separates. Secession crises, as I have already shown, are
notorious for causing highly polarized ethnic bloc voting.

In the first scenario, voting is conducted for Pontiac riding as a
whole. In the second, voting is done on a poll-by-poll basis; each
neighbourhood, in essence, determines the country to which it
shall belong.

In a riding-wide referendum, the riding's 26,000 francophones
(54 percent of Pontiac's total population) would prevail over its
22,000 non-francophones, and the riding would go to Quebec.
Nearly as many persons would have been denied residency in
their country of choice as would have gained it.

Contrast this with the results of a poll-by-poll vote. According
to my calculations, which are based on a probabilistic calculation
of the ethnic breakdown in each poll, fifty-six of the riding's 137
polls would vote to stay in Canada, while eighty-one would vote
to join Quebec. In all, the francophone population remaining in
Canada would only be 5,370, while only 3,500 non-francophones
would be forced to live in Quebec. Seventy percent of the riding's
population would be able to live in the country of its choice, up
from 54 percent under the riding-based referendum formula.[63]

Applied to the whole of Quebec, this formula provides impress-
ive results. If the entire province were to be partitioned on the basis
of poll-by-poll referenda, half a million non-francophones would
be able to continue living in Canada.[64] The population remaining
in Canada would include almost exactly half of the non-francophone population of Quebec. Within Montreal, the neighbourhoods in which the immigrant minorities live are more widely
dispersed than the city's anglophone neighbourhoods, with the
result that a substantial majority of the province's anglophones
would be able to continue living in Canada. On the other hand,
substantially more than half of Quebec's 'allophone' immigrants
would be left in an independent Quebec. As well, only 185,000
francophones (less than 4 percent of Quebec's French-speaking
population) would be left outside the reduced boundaries of the
partitioned state.

The results apply with equal effect in all parts of the province,
as the chart at the end of this chapter shows. In every region of the
province, substantially more anglophones remain in Canada and
significantly more francophones remain in Quebec when polls are

used as the base unit of partition than under any alternative system. If local sovereignty is the only issue, then partition on the basis of individual polls is the only way to go.

There are problems with this formula. A glance at the maps in this chapter reveals that this system would leave Canada with many tiny enclaves. The problem of enclaves will be discussed in detail in Chapter Six, but a few preliminary remarks can be made here. First, the obvious solution to the enclave problem is to legislate it into non-existence. The largest enclave, on Montreal

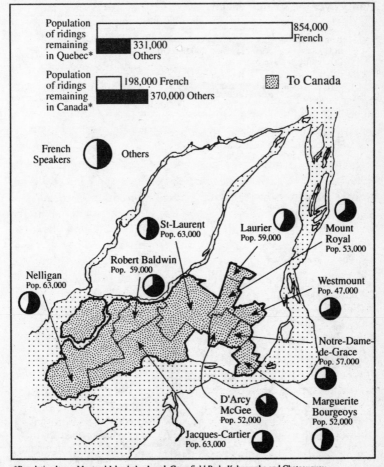

Population of ridings remaining in Quebec*: 854,000 French / 331,000 Others

Population of ridings remaining in Canada*: 198,000 French / 370,000 Others

To Canada

French Speakers / Others

St-Laurent Pop. 63,000

Laurier Pop. 59,000

Mount Royal Pop. 53,000

Robert Baldwin Pop. 59,000

Nelligan Pop. 63,000

Westmount Pop. 47,000

Notre-Dame-de-Grace Pop. 57,000

D'Arcy McGee Pop. 52,000

Marguerite Bourgeoys Pop. 52,000

Jacques-Cartier Pop. 63,000

*Population base: Montreal Island plus Laval, Greenfield Park, Kahnawake and Chateauguay

Montreal partitioned by riding. (Fig. 16)

Island, could be linked to Ontario by a short road corridor (Montreal is only twenty-five miles from the Ontario border).

Smaller enclaves could be turned over to Quebec, since it would be difficult to maintain free access to each one, should the Quebec authorities impose barriers to access. In return, Quebec would be expected to forfeit sovereignty over any enclaves it owned. Since the majority of Quebec's English-speaking population lives in the single large enclave on the West Island, relatively little population would be lost to Quebec through the process of forfeiting sovereignty over the smaller enclaves.

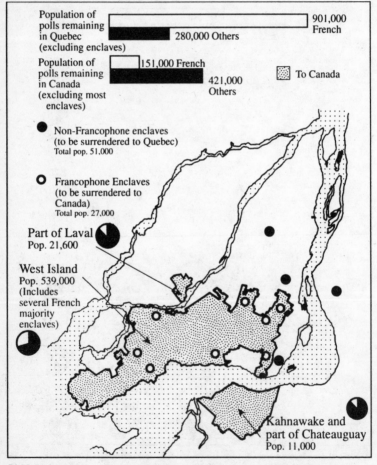

Population base: Montreal Island plus Laval, Greenfield Park, Kahnawake and Chateauguay

Montreal partitioned by poll. (Fig. 17)

A second observation is that the enclave problem is not worse under a poll-based partition model than it is under a system based on individual municipalities. The total non-French population residing in 'unworkably small' enclaves under the poll system is 59,000. Under the municipality-based system this number is 52,000, and includes some fairly important anglophone areas, like Westmount. Only under a riding-based system would the enclave problem be less severe.

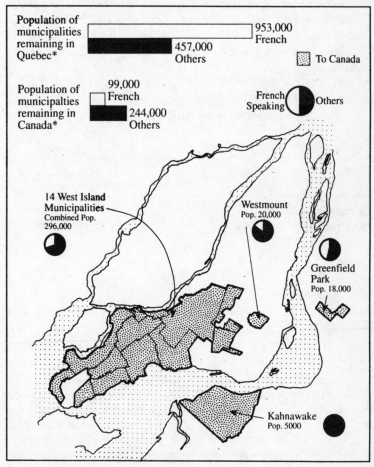

Population base: Montreal Island plus Laval, Greenfield Park, Kahnawake and Chateauguay

Montreal partitioned by municipality. (Fig. 18)

However, even after taking into account the necessity of abandoning small enclaves, the poll-based partition formula still leaves far more people living in their country of choice than does any alternative system. In the end this is what really counts, and what makes the poll-based formula superior to all the others.

SUMMARY

The secret to executing a just and peaceful partition lies in the size of the voting unit. The smaller the units, the better the representation of local majority sentiments. The following chart shows the difference between the four different voting units considered in this chapter:

Population Distribution
Under Various Partition Systems

	Canada		Quebec	
	Franco-phones	Others	Franco-phones	Others
County-based partition	9,000	11,000	5,429,000	1,083,000
Municipality-based partition*	102,000	244,000	5,336,000	850,000
Riding-based partition	198,000	370,000	5,240,000	724,000
Poll-based partition*	185,000	534,000	5,253,000	560,000

* Totals for these categories are based upon the assumption that enclaves (other than the largest enclave in the west end of Montreal, and the exclaves along the American border) will not be permitted to exist. Figures for Canada include the population of French-majority enclaves returned to Canada. Figures for Quebec include the population of English-majority enclaves returned to Quebec. For this reason, the figures in these categories will not match with those in the text of this chapter.

CHAPTER SIX

The Problem of Enclaves

An obvious objection to any sort of partition, and especially to the poll-based system of local votes advocated in this book, is that it would result in the creation of many tiny enclaves of Canadian territory in Quebec. This reservation has been expressed in picturesque terms by Parti Québécois functionary Jean-Paul Servant, who objected to the notion of permitting English-majority areas to remain in Canada, because "It's completely far-fetched. . . . Quebec would be like a piece of Swiss cheese."[65]

In reality, this danger can be easily overcome, if the local referendum formula is carefully planned. A map of the English and French-speaking areas of Quebec reveals that most of Quebec's anglophones and Natives reside in areas which touch on the territory of other provinces. Following partition, these areas would not be enclaves at all, of course. There are six geographically distinct areas in Quebec with large populations of non-francophones, four of which are located on Quebec's borders:

- **West Quebec** (anglophone population: 67,000) lies just north of the Ottawa River and the Ontario border.

- The **North Shore** of the Gulf of St. Lawrence east of Natashquan, dotted with outport communities which are culturally identical to those across the water in Newfoundland, is contiguous with Labrador. At the time of the 1986 census its English-speaking population was 4,070. Even the tiny English-dominated islands called **Entry**

Island and **Grosse Island** in the middle of the Gulf of St.
Lawrence are actually closer to the coasts of Nova Scotia and
Prince Edward Island than they are to the mainland of Quebec. These tiny islands contain a total of less than 800 people,
but 94 percent of this small population is anglophone.

- The vast northern taiga and tundra region called **Nouveau-
  Québec** (Native population: 18,000) is contiguous with
  both Labrador and Ontario, and the aboriginal communities along the Hudson Bay coast maintain close cultural
  links with their fellow Natives on the Ontario Coast, in the
  Belcher Islands, which are part of the Northwest Territories.

- The **Eastern Townships**, which contain 70,000 anglophones,
  are not contiguous with another province, but they do lie
  directly on the northern border of the states of Vermont and
  New York.

- The 11,000 English-speakers on the **Gaspé Peninsula** are
  isolated from the rest of Canada.

- The English-language and immigrant communities in
  Montreal (combined population: 711,000) are isolated from
  Ontario by twenty-five miles of mostly French-populated
  farmland.

Following the River Settlement Pattern

This geographical distribution reflects the fundamental rule governing ethnic patterns of settlement. In Canada as elsewhere, initial
settlement patterns tend to follow waterways. Since lakes, rivers,
and even the open sea are natural avenues of transportation and
communication, people of the same ethnicity will usually be found
on both sides of any body of water. Later, political boundaries will
be created (usually as the result of wars) which will treat these
bodies of water as boundaries. This has the effect of isolating
within foreign territory those minorities that have had the
misfortune to live on the far side of the river or sea from the parent
community.

Often the results of this isolation can be tragic. The poor treatment of the German-speaking Alsatians on the French-owned side
of the Rhine River was one of the causes of the Franco-Prussian
War of 1870. The decision of the Turks in 1923 to expel the Greek

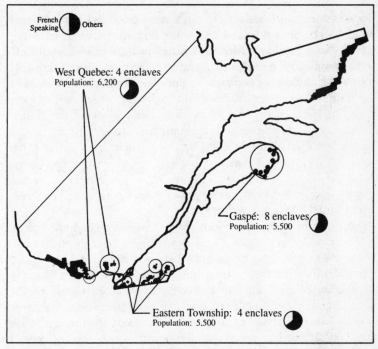

Canadian enclaves in Quebec under a poll-based partition. (Fig. 19)

inhabitants of the Turkish-owned eastern coast of the Aegean Sea resulted in mass slaughter and the dispossession and migration of 1.5 million Greeks from territory that had been part of their homeland for three thousand years.

With the exception of the farm communities of the Eastern Townships, all the non-francophone communities of Quebec have the same kind of water-linked history. The water-borne transportation thesis even explains the existence of anglophone Montreal, which developed because the city was Canada's largest port for two centuries. In the nineteenth century, it was the francophones who were the linguistic minority in Montreal.

Solving the Swiss Cheese Problem

Partitioned on a poll-by-poll basis as I advocate, Quebec would be neither a checkerboard nor a block of Swiss cheese. The pattern that develops when a probabilistic analysis of ethnic voting patterns is done is very much what one might have expected: several large solid blocks of non-francophone territory in places like Pontiac County and west-end Montreal, surrounded by border areas in which some polls go to Canada and some go to Quebec. According to my calculations of probable voting patterns, Canada would be left with several dozen enclaves within the territory of the independent Québécois state, as well as seven exclaves along the United States border. (Exclaves are distinguished from enclaves in that they are not fully surrounded by the territory of a single other state.) A further eight small parcels of territory along the Gaspé coast would be accessible to the rest of Canada only by water. Quebec would have sovereignty over more than a dozen enclaves surrounded by Canadian territory.

Some of these enclaves would be as small as a single poll, with a few hundred residents. Often the ethnic mix in an individual enclave is virtually a 50-50 split between French-speakers and members of other linguistic groups. In total, I calculate that the population of the Canadian enclaves and exclaves (excluding the very large enclave on Montreal Island and the exclaves touching on the Vermont border) to be around 59,000. In these smaller enclaves, around 40 percent of the population is francophone. I calculate the total population of the Quebec-owned enclaves to be around 30,000, of whom about 35 percent are non-French. If all the small Canadian-owned enclaves were to be turned over to Quebec, Canada's net loss of non-francophones from the transaction would be less than 4 percent of the total non-French population of Quebec. If Quebec, in turn, were to surrender its enclaves to Canada, it would actually gain more French speakers than it would lose by the elimination of minor enclaves, due to the larger number of Canadian enclaves it would stand to gain. (The detailed population statistics are compiled in Appendix B at the end of this book.)

It is difficult for democrats and believers in the principle of local self-determination to support this sort of exchange of enclaves. But looking at the issue from the perspective of practicality, it is pretty obvious that it would be costly and aggravating trying to maintain sovereignty over many small discontinuous pieces of territory, particularly since it is possible that residents of the Canadian enclaves could be harassed and blockaded by Québécois nationalist militants following the independence of Quebec, with Canadian police unable to halt this activity without violating Quebec sovereignty.

Since we want to avoid turning over pieces of territory against the will of the residents except when absolutely necessary, the best way to deal with the problem of small enclaves would be to adopt one of the aspects of the Jura model. The 400,000-plus residents of the largest enclave of non-francophone territory—the western half of the island of Montreal, more or less—should be guaranteed the right to remain part of Canada regardless of problems of geographical isolation. This would parallel the special protection offered to the Laufen district in the legislation governing the Jura partition. Laufen, it will be recalled, was so distinctly German that it was guaranteed the right to remain part of the Canton of Berne despite its physical isolation from the rest of the canton. Another parallel to the Jura model would be to permit exclaves of territory which touch upon the boundaries of the United States to remain in Canada. (In the Jura, all exclaves touching upon other cantons were permitted to remain in Berne.) This would protect the rights of the English-speaking population in the Eastern Townships. All other enclaves, whether owned by Canada or by Quebec, would be returned to the surrounding country.

THE ENCLAVE OF MONTREAL

Why the West Island Must be Retained by Canada

Of all the areas likely to become Canadian enclaves completely surrounded by regions voting to secede, only western Montreal is really populous. The West Island's non-francophone community is simply too vast to cast aside, so special arrangements would have to be made for the region's continued membership in Confederation.

Under the local referendum system, most of the parts of Montreal's metropolitan area which voted to stay within Confederation would form a single large enclave surrounded by Quebec territory. This enclave, with a population in excess of 400,000 (more than three times the population of Prince Edward Island), would be economically viable as long as it continued to have unhindered access to the rest of Canada. Maintenance of the right of free road, rail, and air passage to and from Montreal would have to be a non-negotiable condition of any separation treaty, as would unhindered travel and communications between Ontario and the Atlantic provinces. To a certain degree the city's isolation is limited because Dorval Airport is on the West Island, and the St. Lawrence Seaway passes by its south shore.

However, the fact that the West Island enclave would be carved out of territory formerly belonging to Quebec would cause a special problem not faced by the Atlantic provinces. Like West Berlin, west-end Montreal's access to the rest of Canada could be blockaded. I do not believe that the Quebec government would attempt an outright blockade on the 1949 West Berlin model, but it is not difficult to imagine the government refusing to use force to remove nationalist activists blocking the bridges between western Montreal and the mainland. In the summer of 1990 the barricades set up by the Mohawks on the Mercier bridge at Kahnawake showed just how easily access to an island city like Montreal can be cut off by a simple roadblock. Only two bridges connect the West Island to the highways leading to Ottawa and Toronto. If these bridges were seized by nationalist activists, it is doubtful whether the government of the newly independent state of Quebec would have the nerve to use force to clear the protestors out of the way in the service of protecting Canada's continued control over half the territory of Quebec's largest city.

For this reason, Canada needs to have sovereign control over a corridor running from Montreal to the Ontario border. To have transit rights on a corridor that remains under Quebec sovereignty would not be enough, in my opinion, since Canadian authorities would lack the ability to use whatever means are necessary, including riot police, to remove obstructions to free passage.

This does not mean that I favour the creation of a wide swathe of Canadian-owned territory like Ian Ross Robertson's thirty-kilometre-wide corridor between Ontario and New Brunswick. A wide corridor is necessary only if you expect to have to defend it from military attack. Military security was the main reason for the creation of the twentieth century's most infamous corridor—the Polish Corridor, which was created after the First World War and ran through German territory to connect Poland with the Baltic Sea. The Polish Corridor was a little over thirty kilometres wide at its Baltic Sea terminus, and even wider inland. Most of its territory was populated by Germans, who were singularly unhappy about their enforced residence in what they regarded as a foreign country. In the end, the ill will caused by this population's enforced exile was used by Hitler as an excuse for invading Poland.

The population of a corridor connecting Montreal with the Ontario border would be mainly French-speaking, since about two-thirds of the territory traversed by the most logical corridor route is a francophone majority. Since the purpose of a corridor is distinctly not to force any unwilling citizens to remain in Canada, and since there is no danger of a full-scale military offensive against a corridor, the corridor should be made as narrow as possible.

The Colón Corridor: A Model for Montreal?

The problem of isolation from the rest of Canada could best be resolved by creating a corridor on the model of the road corridor that linked the Panamanian city of Colón with the main body of Panamanian territory, in the days when Colón was isolated from its home country.

Colón, located at the mouth of the Panama Canal, is the second largest city in Panama, and is the country's main port on the Atlantic coast. In 1904, the United States signed a treaty with Panama, gaining sovereignty over the zone in which an interoceanic canal was to be built. Colón's location at the eastern terminus of the proposed canal made it necessary to turn the city into an enclave surrounded by American territory. Six miles of Canal Zone territory separated the city from the main body of the country to which it belonged. Eventually the Panamanians found the situation intolerable, and they negotiated a treaty, the *Colón Corridor Convention* of 1950, under which a road corridor was created to link Colón with the rest of the country.

The Corridor was intended to serve purely as an avenue of communications, and in consequence was extremely narrow: 100 feet wide (fifty feet on each side of the road's centre-line) for about half its length, and 200 feet wide for the rest.[66] Although the Corridor was the exclusive territory of the Republic of Panama, its use was restricted under the Convention to transportation and communication functions. The Panamanian government, as sovereign over the Corridor, was expected to provide adequate drainage for runoff, so as to avoid flooding or environmental damage to neighbouring lands within the Canal Zone. As well, 'universal rights of transit' across the Corridor were guaranteed. The Corridor could not be used as a means of cutting off access to the American-owned territory on the far side, since this would have created virtual enclaves.

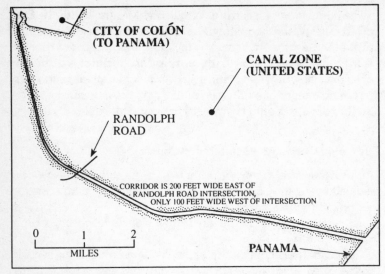

Colón Corridor. (Fig. 20)

The *Colón Corridor Convention* is quite specific in enumerating the limitations on the uses of the corridor. The right of American motorists to drive the length of the Colón Corridor without restriction was guaranteed by the Convention. Americans driving the length of the Corridor would be subject to Panamanian traffic laws and to the Panamanian criminal justice system (should they commit any criminal acts in the course of their transit), but not to other legal restrictions such as Panama's automobile licensing system. The United States retained the right to construct road or rail intersections at any point along the Corridor, or to run sewers or telephone lines across the Corridor.

The arrangements for sovereignty over the point at which the Colón Corridor intersected with a pre-existing American thoroughfare named Randolph Road are described in considerable detail. At this point the Corridor is interrupted by a strip of American territory, the width of the existing Randolph Road right-of-way. American motorists on Randolph Road would never have to leave United States soil, even in the act of crossing the asphalt of the Colón Highway. However, they would be subject at that point to Panamanian traffic laws. Panamanian motorists driving along the Corridor would not be subject to American laws, even in the act of passing through American

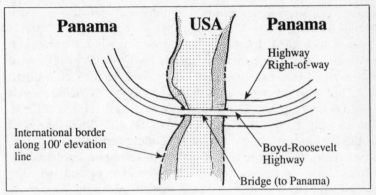

Chagres River intersection. (Fig. 21)

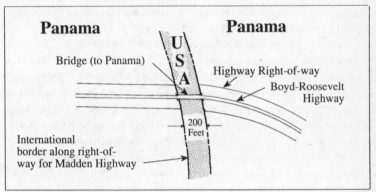

Madden Road intersection. (Fig. 22)

territory as they crossed the Randolph Road right-of-way. In effect, the point of intersection became a tiny rectangle of jointly-administered territory.

The Convention shows a clear preference for the construction of a viaduct or overpass at this point of intersection or at any others that might occur as the Americans built roads across the width of the Corridor. The Convention specifies that in the event of the construction of such an overpass by the Panamanians at the Randolph Road intersection, the overpass would become Panamanian territory and the roadway below would remain American. Thought of in three-dimensional terms, this would have produced a 'tube' of sovereign Panamanian territory passing over American territory—a concept which is initially difficult to grasp, for minds formed by years of thinking of sovereignty as a two-dimensional, flat, and map-oriented concept.

Two such aerial tubes of sovereignty actually did come into existence under the terms of the treaty. The *Colón Corridor Convention* granted Panama sovereignty not only over the Colón Corridor, but also over the entire length of the Boyd-Roosevelt Highway, which runs in a south-easterly direction from Colón to Panama City on the Pacific coast. The route of the Boyd-Roosevelt Highway took it through several protruding peninsulas of American territory along the extremely irregular eastern border of the Canal Zone. At one point a highway bridge passed over the American-owned Chagres River. Elsewhere along the Boyd-Roosevelt Highway, another bridge passed over the American-owned Madden Highway.

Both the Chagres River and the Madden Highway were pre-existing corridors of American sovereignty passing through Panamanian territory. The Madden Highway connected the Madden hydroelectric dam, which provided the electricity to power the Panama Canal's ship locks, with the main body of the Canal Zone. The Chagres River carried runoff from the dam back into Canal Zone territory from the enclave in which Madden Dam was located. Where the Boyd-Roosevelt Highway intersected with these American corridors, it became an airborne tube of sovereign Panamanian territory passing directly over the territory of the United States. The Convention provides a precise description of the international boundary at these intersections. Panama is to have sovereignty over a tube of space conforming exactly to the shape of the bridges, and to retain absolute control over traffic on the bridges. All other sovereign rights are retained by the United States.

A Road Corridor for Montreal

The western tip of the island of Montreal lies only twenty-five miles from the Ontario border if one follows Autoroute 40 to Ottawa, and about thirty-five miles if Autoroute 20 is taken in the direction of Toronto. There is a case for the creation of a corridor on the Colón model along each of these two highways. However, it should be remembered that the real purpose of a corridor is as a sort of insurance policy against blockades. As long as there is one corridor, it will be futile for anyone to blockade the other highway. In consequence, both the highway on Canadian soil and the one that is not would be left open. This eliminates the need for a second corridor. Likewise, I see no need for a corridor to protect the rail lines into Montreal. The main rail lines to the rail yards in the east end of the city must first pass through the west end, so a blockade of trains bound for the Canadian enclave would wind up inconveniencing the Quebec-owned parts of the city as much as the Canadian parts.

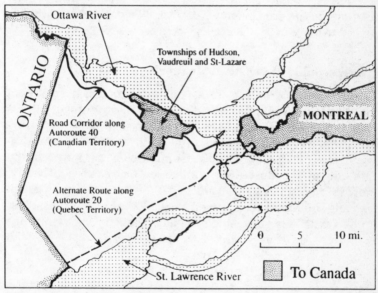

Montreal road corridor. (Fig. 23)

Autoroute 40, which skirts the south shore of the Ottawa River along its twenty-five-mile route, is the logical choice for a corridor. For about a third of its length this route passes through anglophone-majority polls in the townships of Vaudreuil, St-Lazare, and Hudson. These polls together form an enclave of about 5,000 people, which, in the absence of a corridor, would be isolated within Quebec territory and ineligible to remain in Canada. On either side of the enclave, Autoroute 40 enters territory in which francophones form the majority of the local population. Here, the road would be protected by a strip of Canadian territory the width of the existing right-of-way. Autoroute 40 is a four-lane divided highway with cloverleaf on-ramps and off-ramps, so there are no inconvenient intersections like the one the Panamanians encountered at Randolph Road.

The administration of the corridor would require minimal effort, aside from the normal maintenance functions already in place. Depending upon how sticky the Quebec authorities plan on being about customs and immigration protocol, border posts might be necessary at a small number of points along the route where it is possible to exit from the highway. If the Quebec authorities want it, these access points could be shut down entirely. Best of all, the corridor has no population whatsoever. Not one person would be forced to move or to switch allegiances because of its creation.

The Feasibility of a Divided Montreal

A more serious problem, at least on the face of it, is the matter of physically partitioning a world-class city like Montreal, with its complex, integrated economy, transit system, and infrastructure. Philip Resnick, a professor of political science at the University of British Columbia, summarizes the problem by bringing up the most obvious analogy: "One can see it already, now that West Berlin has vanished, West Montreal with a wall skirting University Avenue and Mount Royal and cutting across to Ile Laval!" He goes on to speculate about " . . . moving vans with refugees from Westmount and Notre-Dame-de-Grâce with tales of horror. . . . "[67]

Resnick's rhetoric is extreme, but his point is well taken. Can a city survive and prosper, sliced in half like Berlin was between 1945 and 1989? The answer is yes.

For one thing, it goes without saying that the leadership of an independent Quebec would be considerably more reasonable and open than the East German regime of Erich Honecker. It is not going to erect a wall along St. Lawrence Street or shoot citizens who try to escape to the English-speaking West Island. Indeed, faced with the long-term reality of a divided city, the government in Quebec City is likely, after some preliminary huffing and puffing, to do all it can to ensure that both halves of Montreal prosper. The Montreal region is, after all, the economic heartland of Quebec, and the prosperity of each half of the city will very much depend upon the economic health of the other.

Canada could do its part to make the whole arrangement work by keeping border controls to a minimum. If tens of thousands of

Montrealers are to cross the international boundary twice a day on the way to and from work, border checks of even the most limited sort will have to be avoided. This would require the adoption of at least a few unified policies by Canada and Quebec.

One possible way of achieving this would be to give the residents of the West Island enclave the option of holding a referendum on whether to adopt Quebec's tariff structure, while remaining part of Canada. This would eliminate the need for customs inspections at the border with the Québécois parts of Montreal. This is admittedly an odd-sounding proposal, but there is a precedent for it. Germany and Italy have both opted to permit their enclaves within Swiss territory to adopt the Swiss tariff structure. As a result, persons crossing from the Italian enclave of Campione D'Italia to the Swiss canton of Ticino, by which it is surrounded, or from German-owned Busingen to the canton of Schaffaussen, have only a signpost to inform them that they have left foreign territory and entered Switzerland. On the downside, this arrangement would also mean that Montrealers would have to keep paying the same inflated prices for dairy products and other made-in-Quebec goods that they do now, thanks to the highly protectionist nature of the province's economy.

To judge by the rhetoric of the separatists on the advantages of close economic links under Sovereignty-Association, such limited measures of post-separation unification should not be too difficult to obtain. But even if this failed, Canada could emulate Singapore, which maintains full border controls for most foreigners, but allows Malaysian commuters to enter the country with only about as much fuss and delay as one normally encounters when crossing a toll bridge.

A case can even be made that a partitioned city would be an economic boon to an independent Quebec. According to a recent poll, well over half of Anglo-Quebecers would move out of Quebec if it became independent. If Anglo-Quebecers were provided with the opportunity to continue living in a Canadian enclave after separation, most of them would probably stay. Their skills would continue to benefit the local economy on both sides of the new border, and their investments would continue to provide jobs to residents of the Quebec side of the city and tax revenues for the government of Quebec.

The City-State of Montreal?

Montreal would not be the first internationally-divided city to function effectively. On the Canada-U.S. border, for instance, are Niagara Falls, New York, and Niagara Falls, Ontario, as well as Windsor-Detroit and the twin cities of Sault Ste-Marie, Ontario, and Sault Ste-Marie, Michigan. Hong Kong and Shenzen are economically one city, even though one is a British Crown possession and the other is part of China. Further south in Asia, Singapore and Johor Baharu are twin cities separated by an international boundary.

The Singapore example is perhaps the best one for the purpose of drawing parallels with Montreal. Thousands of workers flood daily into the city-state of Singapore from Johor Baharu, Malaysia, returning home at night to what are, effectively, extra-territorial bedroom communities. (Singapore is located on an island slightly larger than Montreal and is separated from its mainland sister city by a narrow strait.) For reasons of economy some services are partially integrated. Malaysia runs the Singapore railway station, and Singapore's water supply is provided from the Malaysian mainland. Singapore was, incidentally, a state in the Federation of Malaysia until 1965, when it seceded due to irreconcilable differences in ethnic policy between the Chinese-dominated Singapore state government and the Malay-dominated federal government.

The parallels between Singapore and Montreal are so remarkable that former Montreal mayor Jean Drapeau once suggested that the real solution to Quebec's problems was for Montreal to secede from both Canada and Quebec and become the Singapore of North America.68 Of course Drapeau was speaking half-facetiously and did not pursue the idea, but the point is clear.

A final point: no separatist finds it at all upsetting to consider the prospect of Quebec's independence resulting in the partition of Ottawa-Hull—Canada's fourth largest urban area. This indifference is expressed despite the fact that many Ontarians work in Hull and enormous numbers of Quebecers work on the Ontario side of the Ottawa River, usually for the federal government. As the representatives of the Societé d'Aménagement de l'Outaouais explained in a brief to the Bélanger-Campeau Commission,

> The integration of the two sides of the river . . . translates into an important exchange of labour . . . close to 34,000 residents of Quebec work in Ottawa—nearly 33 percent of all the workers in the Outaouais—as opposed to 17,500 Ontarians who

work in Quebec (about 5 percent of the labour force residing in Ottawa).[69]

If, under these circumstances, the partition of Ottawa-Hull presents no insurmountable problems to the Quebec separatists, then surely neither would the partition of Montreal.

The partition of Montreal on the basis of the wishes of local inhabitants of each part of the island would lead to at least a few borderline peculiarities of a sort not encountered in cities like Singapore or West Berlin. The possibility of a few large enclaves exists. At least a few other peculiarities may also be expected. One example is individual city blocks which are internationally divided, with the backyard fence lines forming the international boundary.

The 49th Paradigm

This prospect need not send shivers down anybody's spine. The Canada-U.S. border is full of such anomalies. Canadian houses near Point Roberts on the Pacific coast have backyards which touch on the international boundary; some Canadian householders stack their backyard woodpiles in the United States.

As well, there is an airport whose runway lies partially in Manitoba and partially in the state of Minnesota. An international golf course is situated half in New Brunswick and half in Maine. Visitors to the town of Beebe Plain, Quebec/Beebe Plain, Vermont will find a street that is sliced down the middle by the border, while in Rock Island, Quebec/Derby Line, Vermont, there are several houses which sit astride the line.

Between Friends/Entre Amis, the glossy coffee table book published by the National Film Board in 1976 as a bicentennial birthday gift from the Canadian government to the United States, contains many photographs of houses and other buildings situated partially in one country and partially in the other.[70] A typical descriptive blurb from the book reads:

> [The Bolduc family's] house is on the international border. The kitchen is in Canada, the living room in the United States. The boundary cuts through Ms. Bolduc's own room. Although no routine steps are taken to inspect the houses in which a room is cut by the border, neither furniture nor appliances may be moved across that room, and out of the country in which they were bought, without becoming subject to duty.

Another passage describes the problems faced by farmer Lyle Hurtubise, whose farm lies half in Quebec and half in Vermont:

> At one time, the United States had a duty on imported hay, and Mr. Hurtubise used only in Canada the hay that he grew in Canada. Custom regulations have changed, and Mr. Hurtubise is now allowed to feed Canadian hay to his United States cattle.

Other photographs show a theatre in which the audience sits in the United States while performers sing and dance in Canada, a pool hall that lies on the border (the cigarette vending machine is located in New York State, to take advantage of the lower tobacco taxes), and a stretch of the Saint John River on which recreational skaters dart from Maine to New Brunswick and back without suffering apparent harm.

Perhaps the best description of the common-sense attitude which governs the dealings of the Canadian and the United States authorities on such matters is provided by the blurb which accompanies a photograph of Georges and Cécile Béchard staring out, respectively, from the Canadian and American windows of their modest shingle-covered home:

> The Béchards' house is built on the Quebec-Maine line. It is the present policy of the International Boundary Commission to allow no new structures, for dwelling or other purposes, to be built on the border, but no existing building is affected unless Customs officers have seized contraband in it, and a conviction has been obtained. . . .

These examples are cited merely to show that unconventional border arrangements can lead to perfectly practical and tolerable solutions. The border which would be produced as a result of a partition based on majority votes within political divisions such as municipalities or polls would not contain any situations as peculiar as the ones described above. Still, to make the point that under circumstances of goodwill it is possible to carry on life in the most peculiar of political arrangements, a few more exotic examples from overseas can be cited.

Enclaves Around the World

Numerous enclaves exist in the world today, and function perfectly well. The Spanish town of Llivia in the Pyrenees Mountains is completely surrounded by French territory. India owns two towns completely surrounded by Bangladesh territory. The tiny republic of San Marino is an enclave surrounded by Italy, while the Kingdom of Lesotho is surrounded by South African territory. The German town of Busingen and the Italian town of Campione d'Italia are located in enclaves entirely surrounded by Swiss territory.

Within Switzerland itself, nearly every canton possesses sovereignty over chunks of non-contiguous territory. Eleven of these territorial possessions are true enclaves (land belonging to one canton which is completely surrounded by the territory of another), while an additional twelve are exclaves. A further four Swiss enclaves are isolated from their respective home canton by lakes and can be reached only by passing through waters which belong to another canton.

To a certain extent, Switzerland's geographical peculiarities do not matter, since all the cantons are today part of one country, but it should be remembered that most Swiss cantons were at one time independent countries. The enclaves date mostly from this period, and many were created during periods of strife, when partitioning territories along religious or ethnic lines seemed to make more sense than forcing minority populations to flee their homes or adopt a hated religion.

Baarle-Hertog

The most fascinating example of a fully functional enclave lies on the Dutch border with Belgium. The town of Baarle-Hertog in the southern Netherlands looks ordinary when viewed from the air. A look at a municipal political map reveals, however, that much of the town is located on Belgian territory. The Belgian part of the town is called Baerle-Duc and takes the form of twenty-two enclaves of different shapes and sizes, each of which is entirely surrounded by Dutch territory.[71] The smallest enclaves are so tiny that they cannot hold an entire house. As a result, many houses are located partially on Belgian and partially on Dutch soil.

Mail is delivered by the Dutch postal service to houses where the front door is in the Netherlands and by the Belgian post office to houses where the front door is in Belgium, but this is further complicated by the fact that some front doors are bisected by the border. Even more confusing, some of the larger enclaves of Belgian territory contain sub-enclaves of Dutch land, each of which is

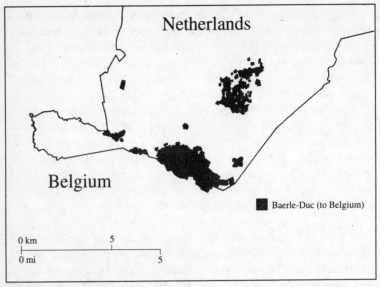

The town of Baarle-Hertog. (Fig. 24)

completely cut off from the rest of the country by the surrounding chunk of Belgian territory.

A political map of the town looks like a satirist's vision of what would happen to Quebec if every household were able to choose the country to which it would belong. The whole town would be completely non-functional if the Belgian and Dutch authorities did not have enough good sense and good humour to realize that bureaucratic stuffiness over the etiquette of border-crossing helps nobody. As painful as the issue of partition is, a formula based on very small units will ensure that good sense and perhaps even good humour will eventually prevail here too.

SUMMARY

If Quebec is partitioned, there will be small enclaves in West Quebec, the Gaspé, and the Eastern Townships. West Montreal will constitute an even larger enclave. Canadians and Quebecers have reacted negatively toward the idea of enclaves, fearing that sovereign territory will be difficult to access or defend. Most Canadians and Quebecers do not realize that enclaves exist, and function well, on the North American continent and around the world.

The following rules must be followed when dealing with the idea of enclaves in Quebec:

- **Do what is practical.**
  Common sense should dictate whether an enclave can exist or not. Small, isolated Canadian enclaves are indefensible and too costly to maintain, so they may have to be abandoned to Quebec. The exceptions to this rule are the parts of the Eastern Townships that border on the United States (since the U.S. provides an alternate means of access) and the Island of Montreal (since its non-French population is too large to abandon).

- **A divided Montreal can be made workable.**
  A divided Montreal is totally feasible. It would be helpful if the governments of the two new countries co-operate to make practical arrangements for Montreal's shared infrastructure and for ease of transportation between the two halves of the international city, in order that the economic strength of the city not be diminished.

- **Use a road corridor to connect Montreal with Ontario.**
  Arrange guaranteed access to the Canadian enclave in Montreal with a corridor of sovereign Canadian territory.

CHAPTER SEVEN

Quebec's Native Peoples

December 1990 marked the 100th anniversary of the Battle of Wounded Knee and the end of the Indian wars in the United States. In Quebec, however, the struggle may be far from over. During the second half of 1990, worldwide attention was focused upon the unexpected outbreak of armed violence on two Mohawk reserves in Quebec.

The dispute first made the news in July, when the residents of the Kanesatake reserve near the small town of Oka just west of Montreal refused to vacate a piece of land they had seized in March, after it had been slated for development as part of a golf course. The Mohawks claimed they owned the land, since, they maintained, it had never been signed over to the Crown by treaty. The unusual measure of seizing the land by force was partly a response to frustration with the court system, which the Mohawks felt was ignoring their claims. It was also partly a result of their frustration with the media, which had been totally unresponsive to their previous non-violent protests.

On July 11, a force of 100 officers of the Sûreté du Québec attempted, with the aid of assault rifles, tear gas and concussion grenades, to extricate the Mohawks. They fought back, and one policeman was shot and killed. The police backed off.

In the wake of this confrontation, Mohawks elsewhere protested the decision by the provincial authorities to respond to force with force. Later the same day, the residents of Kahnawake reserve, located just south of Montreal, closed off access to the

Mercier Bridge, which forms the main link between that city and its suburbs to the south. This was an openly illegal and political action, designed to make life unpleasant for thousands of commuters.

Shortly afterwards, the Fifth Brigade of the Canadian army was called in to keep the peace at the reserves. Robert Bourassa, who had just authorized the conduct of a study (the Allaire Report) advocating *de facto* independence for his province, saw no contradiction in calling out the Canadian army to restrain Natives who were thinking out loud about *de facto* independence from Quebec. International observers were dispatched to watch the crisis in the heart of the country that probably exports more United Nations observers per capita than any other nation on earth.

There is a substantial potential for conflict in aboriginal Quebec as the province moves towards independence. Quebec is home to several increasingly self-aware aboriginal nations, each of which is demanding recognition of an inherent right of self-determination. This presumably includes the right to withdraw aboriginal territory from Quebec in the event of separation. The position that appears to be generally accepted among Natives is that such lands include wide swathes of territory presently inhabited by whites, or else containing valuable fixed assets.

Not surprisingly, the Québécois nationalist position on Native rights is somewhat less generous. In the nationalist view, Native self-determination must take a back seat to Quebec's search for sovereignty. The yawning gulf between these two positions provides more potential for trouble than any other issue that a newly independent Quebec will face. Some of the possible flashpoints are in southern Quebec (notably the Mohawk reserves at Oka and Kahnawake), but the greatest potential for violence is in the North, at James Bay. Here the multi-billion dollar aspirations of one of the world's most powerful public utilities come into direct conflict with the cultural survival of Quebec's wealthiest and most effectively organized aboriginal nation.

Who are Quebec's Aboriginal Nations?

There are 60,000 Natives in Quebec, about 10 percent of whom are Inuit. The Quebec government officially recognizes the existence of eleven aboriginal nations on its soil. Only three of these nations (the Cree, the Inuit, and the Naskapi) have signed comprehensive land agreements; the others have unresolved legal claims to variously-

sized portions of the province's landmass. Until these claims have
been resolved, it will be legally impossible for Quebec to take the
disputed lands with it out of the Canadian confederation.

The geographical scope of this problem is outlined in the sub-
mission made to the Bélanger-Campeau Commission by Konrad
Sioui, a member of the Huron nation, and the regional head for
Quebec of the Assembly of First Nations:

> The Inuit of Quebec, the James Bay Cree and the Naskapi of
> Northeastern Quebec occupy land, under treaties, which ac-
> counts for approximately one-half the land mass of Quebec.
> The Montagnais, Attikameks, Algonquins, Micmacs, Mo-
> hawks, Abenakis, Malécites and my own people, the Huron-
> Wendat nation, have aboriginal titles to about one-third of the
> balance and we also occupy many areas designated as reserves
> under the Canadian *Indian Act*.[72]

At present, there are eight aboriginal nations within Quebec
that have outstanding or unsettled land claims. Some of these
nations, such as the Hurons of the Quebec City region and the
Micmacs of the Gaspé, inhabit thickly populated regions and are
not in a strong bargaining position. However, some of the claims
of the northern nations are considerably more forceful. In the
northeastern part of the province, the Montagnais and Attikamek
nations have not yet signed treaties surrendering any portion of
their territory to the Quebec government. In 1989 the Algonquins
of the Pontiac-Temiskaming-Abitibi region in western Quebec
filed a comprehensive land claim to nearly 80,000 square miles of
mostly unincorporated territory. (The combined territory of the
three Maritime provinces is 52,000 square miles.) There is even an
outstanding claim to a portion of northern Quebec by the Innu of
Labrador, who do not have any settlements on Quebec lands, but
who have traditionally used some of the territory near the border
for nomadic hunting and foraging activities.

Realistically, it will be impossible to draw a definitive border
between Quebec and Canada until these claims have been settled.
Once this has been done, the lands belonging to each aboriginal
nation could become part of the territory of either Canada or of the
independent state of Quebec, as the majority within the relevant
aboriginal nation chooses. Such a solution would almost certainly
be acceptable to the Native communities. Unfortunately, it does not
appear that this arrangement would be acceptable to the Quebec

government, which is adamant that the Natives must follow the Québécois majority into independence or into whatever other arrangement the government in Quebec City negotiates with Ottawa.

This does not, to be sure, make the Natives into automatic allies of the Canadian side in a future territorial dispute. Frustration at the federal government's unwillingness to take his nation's claim seriously has prompted one Algonquin Chief, Richard Kistabish, to indicate that he would support Quebec sovereignty, provided that Native peoples be given the opportunity to be partners in the sovereignty process.[73]

The Québécois Nationalist Position on Native Self-Determination

It would be unfair to suggest that Quebec's nationalists have not come a long way over the past decade on the issue of Native self-determination. On the other hand, it has to be added that they started from a position of spectacular insensitivity. In 1976, Parti Québécois ideologist Jacques Brossard declared that Quebec's Native peoples did not have the right of self-determination because:

> As far as I can see, they do not appear to be "a people" in the sense of the United Nations charter, due to the following facts:
> 1. Their small number (18,000 Inuit and 300,000 Indians in Canada, constituting 1.5 percent of the total population; 3,800 Inuit and 32,000 Indians in Quebec, constituting 0.5 percent of the total population) [the Native population of Quebec has roughly doubled since this was written];
> 2. Their wide territorial dispersion (across both Canada and Quebec); and
> 3. Their subdivision into diverse ethnicities.[74]

By 1983, the views of the Parti Québécois had matured considerably. In that year, the provincial cabinet adopted a statement of principle recognizing the right of aboriginal nations to control their own lands, as long as such control was understood not to "signify sovereign rights that could affect Quebec's territorial integrity."[75]

Two years later, the provincial legislature voted to recognize the existence of ten aboriginal nations on Quebec soil. The Liberals, who were then in opposition, voted against the resolution. The Liberals appear to have modified their position, since in 1987 the

new Bourassa government added an eleventh aboriginal nation to
this list.

At its policy convention in January 1991, the Parti Québécois
went further, offering to create 'a new social contract' between the
aboriginal nations and a future sovereign Québécois state. In rhetoric at least, the Parti Québécois resolution recognizes the equality
of the aboriginal nations with the Québécois nation. Specifics of the
resolution include the promise that the constitution of an independent Quebec would guarantee the right of aboriginal nations to
establish governments with substantial powers over taxation, citizenship, education, language and culture, health, economic planning, management of the environment, and management of natural
resources. As well, the Natives are promised the right to:

> ... their own responsible governments, empowered, albeit
> gradually for some, to govern the lands they now possess or
> occupy such as the Indian reserves, Native settlements, Cate-
> gory 1 lands [under the James Bay settlement], as well as such
> territories as may be ceded back to them following negotia-
> tions with the Quebec government.[76]

The resolution continues on to condemn those forms of environmental degradation likely to have the strongest impact upon Natives: clear-cutting, some types of mining, and even "thoughtless
hydroelectric development." Special aboriginal electoral districts
are proposed, in order to boost Native representation in the National Assembly.

On paper at least, this is the most generous aboriginal policy set
forth anywhere in Canada by a political party with a realistic
chance of gaining power. The main problem with the plan is that
the Parti Québécois, and Quebec politicians in general, suffer from
a huge credibility gap with the province's Native communities.
The Natives simply do not believe the rhetoric to be sincere.

This gap is partly the result of the residual bad feelings from the
standoffs at Oka and at Kahnawake's Mercier Bridge in the summer of 1990. The Natives are suspicious that if put to the test by
future conflicts between Québécois nationalism and aboriginal
aspirations, future Quebec governments will not hesitate to set
aside their generous promises and crush the Natives with physical
force. This is perhaps a misapprehension, but it is not aided by the
off-the-cuff pronouncements of Quebec's political leaders. Six
months after his party had passed its resolutions on Native self-

government, Jacques Parizeau stated in an interview in *Saturday Night* that an independent Quebec would need a military of its own "in order to keep our bridges open."[77]

Why English Canada Cannot Turn Its Back on Quebec's Natives

As Quebec moves towards independence, English-speaking Canada will inevitably be dragged headlong into any dispute, peaceful or otherwise, involving the province's aboriginal nations. Public opinion surveys in the English-speaking parts of the country reveal an overwhelming desire to settle aboriginal land claims and to compensate the Natives for past injustices. This popular mood, coupled with the generalized sense of anger and betrayal toward French Canada that would probably prevail in the event of separation, would make it almost impossible for federal politicians to ignore the entreaties of Native groups requesting the right to have their ancestral homelands remain under the Canadian flag.

In truth, it would be a dereliction of our responsibilities as a nation for Canadians not to respond favourably to such entreaties—even though it is clear that the ultimate loyalty of most Natives in Quebec is not to Canada, but to their own ancestral nations. For the post-separation Canadian state, the danger lies in failing to anticipate that such requests are likely to be made. Canada could then be forced to choose sides in a series of Québécois-Native disputes in which both antagonists take up extreme and irreconcilable positions. The trick for Canada, therefore, will be to develop and set in place an institutional apparatus that will prevent this from happening.

Already the idea of playing Canada and Quebec against each other as a way of maximizing the benefits accruing to his own community has occurred to at least one aboriginal leader. In the course of a public question-and-answer session with the federal minister of Constitutional Affairs in November 1991, a chief from the Mohawk reserve at Oka inquired of Joe Clark if he would be willing to use force against Quebec in a separation crisis in order to protect the Mohawk nation's rights of self-determination. Clark avoided a direct response by indicating that force is not the Canadian way of resolving disputes, and the incident died away with fairly limited press coverage. But the hat had been dropped. The federal government must now make it clear that violence will not work to the Natives' advantage. The longer the government delays in delivering this message, the greater the potential that extreme partisans of the aboriginal cause may commit some rash act against Quebec in the hope of then being able to hide behind the petticoats of the Canadian Armed Forces. It would then be the military that would pay the cost in treasure (and perhaps in blood) of keeping the peace between the rival nationalisms of the Québécois and the Natives.

The Solution: A Fast Track for Aboriginal Land Claims

The most obvious solution is to speed up the process by which unresolved land claims are adjudicated. The oft-exaggerated claims of many aboriginal nations cover most of Quebec's territory when they are added together (some of the Mohawks even claim the Island of Montreal). As a package the claims are completely unacceptable to the majority of Quebecers, who are not nearly as favourably disposed towards Natives as is English Canada. For the aboriginal nations to present these claims at the time that the borders of an independent Quebec are being set is to invite a flat refusal to negotiate. Events would presumably go downhill from there.

A far superior idea would be to return to the concept, already discussed in Chapter Four, of a comprehensive piece of federal legislation governing secession. One provision of the secession law would be the requirement that treaties be signed by each of Quebec's aboriginal nations *in advance* of secession. A method of binding arbitration would have to be specified to expedite the process of signing treaties, and to ensure that stalling tactics would not be available to any party in the negotiation process. After a certain date following a 'Yes' vote in a province-wide referendum (but before independence is declared), all unresolved disputes would be turned over to a judicial body. This could be the Supreme Court of Canada, a specially-appointed arbitrator, or even the International Court in The Hague.

I do not foresee any of the aboriginal nations attempting to drag their feet on signing treaties, since it is clearly an advantage to them to have the option of accepting offers from two competing states—an option which expires with Quebec's independence. If there is any danger under this arrangement, it is that Canada and some of the aboriginal nations will sign treaties that are excessively generous in awarding territory to these nations. The Canadian government, after all, has nothing to lose in offering vast tracts of land from a departing Quebec to one or another of the aboriginal nations, and then inviting that nation to take the land and rejoin Canada.

The main role of binding arbitration, therefore, would be to determine the justice of such awards. Quebec would have the right to appeal and to offer its own alternative treaties, which might well be less generous. If the arbitrator were to conclude that Canada had been making unreasonable offers and to rule on this basis in favour of any of the deals offered by Quebec, the federal government would be required under the provisions of the secession law to withdraw its treaty offer to the aboriginal nation in question. That nation would be faced with the prospect of joining Quebec under the terms of the treaty already offered by the Quebec government, or else waiting until after independence and attempting to negotiate anew with the Quebec government. This final option would essentially return the nation in question to the situation that exists today, in which everything rests upon the sincerity of the Quebec government in its desire to satisfy Native aspirations once it has achieved independence.

This is a fair procedure designed to protect the legitimate (although conflicting) interests of both the Québécois and the aboriginal nations. The law is emphatically not designed as a way of letting Canada keep as much Quebec territory as possible. Canada's role under the law is not to provide a rival claim to either Québécois or Native interests, but purely to keep the peace and ensure that justice rather than brute strength is the prevailing factor in the resolution of Native land claims. If the end result of such a process is to allow all the aboriginal nations to peaceably and willingly join an independent Quebec with their inherent rights respected and guaranteed, then Canada too will have come out of the proceedings a winner, with its conscience intact and its moral and historical duty towards Quebec's Native peoples complete.

Negotiating Treaties with "A Knife at the Throat"

In a worst-case scenario under this law, the Quebec government might refuse to deal at all with the Natives under the time constraints imposed by the secession bill. Such a refusal would be full of irony, given the tight schedule that the government of Quebec has imposed on the rest of Canada in negotiating a new constitutional deal, under threat of secession. But since consistency has never been an important factor in disputes between nations, the claim that Quebec is being forced to negotiate aboriginal treaties with a "knife at the throat" (to use Léon Dion's description of the tactic presently being employed against English Canada) might be used as a way of refusing to deal at all with the Natives.

The legislation I am proposing can be made to take this possibility into account. As in any good piece of hard-nosed legislation, there must be a willingness to take punitive action to back up the measured reasonableness of this law. Under the circumstances just described, and assuming that the Quebec government refuses in addition to submit alternative draft treaties to the arbitrator as provided for in the legislation, the federal government would have the legal right to negotiate whatever treaties, however outlandish, with the Natives, and to enforce Canadian and aboriginal sovereignty over these lands as it sees fit. In the interests of not provoking a violent reaction from the Quebec government, Ottawa would still, of course, be well-advised to be sensible in its concessions to the Natives.

This option would not be desirable, but it would still be preferable to the likely outcome of the federal government's present policy of silence, which may encourage some of the more militant Natives to take matters into their own hands as the Mohawk Warriors did in the summer of 1990.

The Treaty Nations

Three of the aboriginal nations in Quebec have already signed comprehensive land treaties. The futures of these nations will have to be determined within the context of these treaties. Two of the Nations (the Inuit and the Naskapi) seem relatively satisfied with their treaties. The third Nation (the Cree) are very unhappy with their treaty.

In the two situations where a workable and widely accepted treaty is in force, the logical solution would appear to be to allow a majority vote in each reserve or community to determine the country to which that reserve or community would adhere. Depending on the choice made, rights and obligations specified under the treaties would then be assumed by either Canada or Quebec. As things stand, it seems likely that each of the nations in question will prefer to cast its lot with Canada rather than with Quebec. Therefore it is up to the Quebec government to win over these nations by making itself seem more attractive—perhaps by offering to renegotiate existing treaties on a more generous basis, or instituting ironclad protections for Native rights in the constitution of a sovereign Quebec.

Even among the treaty Natives, there are special circumstances specific to each nation that will require individual attention. This is particularly the case with the Cree nation, which has indicated significant dissatisfaction with the *James Bay and Northern Quebec Agreement*, the treaty it signed with the Bourassa government in the 1970s. There is even some indication that the Cree do not consider the Agreement to still be valid.

SPECIAL PROBLEMS OF THE TREATY NATIONS

The Inuit

The Inuit of northern Quebec are unique among Canada's Native peoples in having agreed to sign a treaty that does not give them reservation lands and place them under exclusive federal jurisdiction. One of the long-term results of the *James Bay and Northern Quebec Agreement*, to which the Inuit are signatories, has been the creation of the 'territory' of Nunavik, a vast Inuit-majority regional municipality including all of the province's lands north of the 55th parallel. This territory, which is about the size of Alberta, has a population of only 7,000 people who live in fourteen villages along the region's northern and western coasts. The Inuit form over 90 percent of Nunavik's population.

The municipal model employed in Nunavik was chosen by the Inuit as preferable to the Reserve model used by most aboriginal nations. The 'territorial' government of Nunavik exercises control over a much larger area than do any of the reserve councils elsewhere in Quebec, but its control is limited to largely municipal functions. And unlike the reserves, which are under federal jurisdiction alone, Nunavik is a full-fledged part of Quebec, and fully subject to Quebec law; unlike the reserve governments, which are racial in character and open only to members of the appropriate aboriginal nation, the Nunavik government is open to all. Non-Natives can move to Nunavik, live there, and run for public office on the territorial/municipal council.

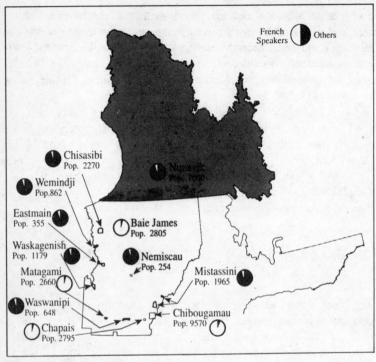

Northern Quebec. (Fig. 25)

The problem in Nunavik is deciding which unit of division to use in holding a local referendum on whether to secede from Quebec. Nunavik itself could serve as a single vast unit of partition, with a vote of the majority of its residents determining the fate of the entire region. The advantage of this system is that it is simple and straightforward. As well, it would ensure that the entire Inuit nation would remain within or depart from Quebec as a single entity. The importance to the Inuit of this internal unity is revealed by a comment made by the Inuit leader, Senator Charlie Watt, as he addressed the Belanger-Campeau Commission on the prospect of Quebec's separation:

> Some Commissioners may be aware that the Inuit of Quebec have been solidifying their ties with fellow Inuit in the rest of Canada, Greenland, Alaska, and even the USSR. This is especially important in relation to the Northwest Territories and Labrador where Nunavik Inuit have many relatives and close friends. Thus, a new arrangement for Quebec based solely on

a South-South relationship between itself and the rest of Canada will be incomplete. Any proposals for Quebec's political and constitutional future will have to address the North-North relationship between Nunavik and the Northwest Territories and Labrador.[78]

However, there is a difficulty with this solution. Three of Nunavik's fourteen communities claim never to have given their consent to the *James Bay and Northern Quebec Agreement*, and in consequence do not recognize the legal existence of Nunavik territory/municipality. It would probably be illegal, or at least illegitimate, to expect these communities to accept the decision of a majority in a political division from which they consider themselves exempt.

Perhaps a better solution for the purpose of a local referendum would be to take advantage of the fact that each of Nunavik's fourteen villages is coterminous with a poll for the provincial riding of 'Ungava.' Under a poll-based formula, each village would be able to vote individually whether to stay in Canada or Quebec.

It is conceivable—but unlikely—that some communities would vote to remain in Canada, while others would choose to join Quebec. In this case, the logical solution would be to divide the unincorporated lands that form about 95 percent of Nunavik's territory between the relevant villages on the basis of a judicial interpretation of the historical land claims of each village. This would not really add complexity or confusion to the situation, since the process of adjudicating between conflicting aboriginal land claims in Nunavik cannot be avoided at any rate. The Inuit of the Belcher Islands, which rest in the middle of Hudson Bay and are part of the Northwest Territories, have asserted a historical claim to certain rights along this coastal region. They are presently negotiating with the Inuit of northern Quebec on this matter.

The Cree

The Cree of James Bay have come a long way since the 1970s when they first faced down the provincial government over Phase I of the James Bay Project. They won an enormous financial settlement from Quebec City over that confrontation, as well as a sense of enmity that has not been eased by the successful Cree-led campaign last year to prevent or at least delay the construction of James Bay Phase II on the Great Whale River.

On the subject of Quebec independence, the Cree have upped the stakes considerably. Chief Billy Diamond has been quoted in a recently released book as saying "I can guarantee you that there will be violent confrontation" if Cree sovereignty is not addressed by an independent Quebec.[79] Diamond's comments come at the end of a year in which violence was hinted at by other chiefs, including Ted Moses, the Cree representative at the United Nations Working Group on Indigenous Nations. In July Moses informed a Geneva meeting of the Group that "should Quebec unilaterally declare sovereignty, it is not likely that indigenous people will passively surrender their lands and rights to the new state. A conflict will occur that, like it or not, will involve the most fundamental issues of international law."[80]

English Canadian observers, delighted to find someone who will actually stand up to the colossus of Québécois nationalism, have made careful note of the strength of the Cree position. McGill University professor William Watson has taken a page from René Lévesque's book and observed that it would be easy for the Cree to blow up the transmission towers that march through hundreds of miles of Cree territory on their way from the banks of the La Grande River to New York State.[81] (As provincial minister of energy in the 1960s, René Lévesque warned that if Quebec's permission were not gained in advance of their construction, transmission towers carrying electricity across Quebec territory from Churchill Falls in Labrador could be blown up.)

At first glance, the Cree appear to have everything going their way in their search for self-government. They are a distinct, cohesive ethnic group, as much a nation by United Nations standards as Quebec itself. Their experience in negotiating the implementation of Phase I of the James Bay project has taught them how to deal with overbearing officials and supercilious bureaucrats. The brilliant campaign against the Great Whale Project has made them the darlings of the American media. They have produced a sophisticated leadership. Thanks to the first James Bay agreement, they are also reasonably wealthy.

The tide of history is flowing in the Crees' direction. The implosion of Yugoslavia and the Soviet Union has given legitimacy to the notion of independence for the smallest and most obscure of nations. If it is no longer absurd to talk of an independent Ossetia, Bashkiria, or Chechen-Ingushetia, why not also grant the Cree the right to decide, at the very least, whether they prefer Canada over Quebec?

At a superficial level, even geography seems to be on the side of the Cree. Located far north of the St. Lawrence heartland of Quebec, they are not hemmed in on all sides by white people, like the Mohawks of Oka and Kahnawake, or the Huron of Wendake. The vast Cree homeland, on which they still retain extensive hunting and fishing rights, extends over about one-third of Quebec's landmass, an easily detachable section lying between the Inuit-inhabited northern third and the white-populated southern third.

As well, there is a compelling moral case for Cree self-determination. The construction of the first phase of the James Bay project resulted in the flooding of many traditional hunting grounds and the mercury poisoning of some waterways. The result was a reduction of the work-space available to the Cree and, in essence, a boost in unemployment. Trapped at home with nothing to do, the Cree have, by their own account, turned to the raising of large families as the only alternate form of meaningful activity.

The Cree population is expanding at Third World rates, due largely to perverse incentives imposed by the provincial government. The population situation is made worse by the Quebec government's policy of paying $7,500 bonuses to parents upon the birth of their third baby and each subsequent child. This policy does not appear to be particularly effective in increasing family sizes in francophone Quebec, where the bonus only partly offsets the high cost of giving up a dual income. But among the Cree, who have been cut off from most forms of gainful activity and are now increasingly unable to carry on their traditional economic pursuits, the bonuses are considerably more attractive. "Indians are having babies because it's the only thing Quebec will pay us to do,"[82] says Matthew Coone-Come, leader of the Grand Council of the Crees and himself a father of five.

The situation seems likely to get much worse if the Quebec government proceeds with the Great Whale Project (and further into the future, if it proceeds with the massive Rupert-Broadback-Nottaway Project, which would be even larger than Phase I of the James Bay Project). These projects would destroy much of what remains of the Crees' traditional hunting grounds, even as their population continues to expand. Coone-Come is clearly unnerved by this situation:

> The white man looks at us and says our population is growing. But we look at the situation and realize that the land is shrink-

ing, that there just won't be enough land for the Cree to survive.[83]

What The North Means To Quebec

The concerns of the Cree are so compelling, and their determination to gain control of their own future so strong, that it is unimaginable that they could be forced to stay peacefully within an independent Quebec. However, they will have to overcome a series of enormous obstacles faced by no other indigenous nation in Quebec. For one thing, the James Bay Agreement, to which their nation is a signatory, gives away many of their rights to these lands. In return for this signature, the Cree nation received $135 million, which has mostly been spent and could not be repaid. They could not afford to repay the provincial government even if the James Bay Agreement had a refund clause. The Cree argue that Quebec has since violated the terms of the agreement, but even if this is true it is probably not sufficient cause to render the treaty legally void. In consequence, most of the ancestral Cree land is firmly under the sovereignty of Quebec.

Moreover, contrary to myth, northern Quebec is full of French people. The population in the territory transferred to Quebec in 1898 and 1912 is currently over 80 percent French-speaking. The part of the North that traditionally belonged to the Cree today contains more French-Canadians than Natives. The North also contains much of Quebec's wealth, including of course the massive James Bay hydroelectric project, which is the pride of Quebec's bureaucratic 'New Class' and a symbol of the strength and independence of Quebec society. It is unlikely that this section of the province could be recovered from Quebec peacefully.

Quebec's 'Graceful Vaulted Arch'

English Canadians—and probably the Cree as well—are mostly unaware of the almost mythological status that hydroelectricity in general, and James Bay in particular, have in the Québécois national self-image. As far back as the pre-Duplessis era of the 1920s, hydro was the one area in which rural, semi-literate Quebec could pride itself on leading the world. That this leadership is based on nothing more than the good fortune of having a large supply of rivers has never dimmed hydro's lustre in the public mind.

The construction of Hydro-Québec's first megaproject, the 3700 megawatt Manicouagan hydroelectric project in the late 1960s, created a province-wide sense of euphoria. Conrad Black gives a sense of the emotional power of this megaproject in a passage from his biography of Maurice Duplessis:

> This costly and graceful vaulted-arch dam, Manic 5 as it was called, 4300 feet long and 660 feet high . . . became a popular symbol of the nationalistic not to say narcissistic Quebec created by the so-called Quiet Revolution of the sixties. A "Manic" automobile and "Manic" cigarettes flourished briefly, more aptly named than their zealous creators probably imagined.[84]

But the scale of the Manicouagan Project pales compared to *Le Chantier de la Baie James*. Phase One (that is, the completed part) of James Bay is, and perhaps always will be, the largest hydroelectric project in the world. To complete it, fifteen massive dams and innumerable dikes were constructed and some rivers were completely redirected. New reservoirs were created, one of them a third as large as Lake Ontario, on what had previously been dry land. $13.7 billion was spent on the construction of the project.

Today, the project generates over 10,000 megawatts of electricity, and pumps $2.02 billion dollars annually into the Quebec treasury. James Bay is one of the primary reasons why Hydro-Québec is the province's largest non-tax source of revenue; the generating stations along James Bay's La Grande River account for 46 percent of Hydro-Québec's total production.[85] In short, the government of Quebec will not be parted easily—or perhaps even peacefully—from James Bay.

Those outside Quebec who note that the region was a two-part gift from long-dead federal prime ministers looking to win a few votes in the province are correct, on a technical level, but they are missing the point. Quebec will not part willingly with James Bay, and attempts to simply seize it will arouse the whole province. Canadians forget too easily that it was the division of fixed assets between the Union and Confederate governments that started the American Civil War. To argue that Canada is carrying out this division in an attempt to help a small imperilled people like the Crees is likely to stir as much sympathy in nationalist circles as the arguments of the radical abolitionists did in the American South as the first shells started falling on Fort Sumpter.

James Bay Power Project: Career Maker, Career Breaker

Perhaps even more important than its economic significance is the role that James Bay has played in the careers of Quebec's most important politicians. Duplessis's skillful handling of the hydro development issue was one of the primary reasons for his extraordinarily long and successful political career in mid-century. Nationalization of hydro in 1962 made energy minister René Lévesque into a cultural hero and ensured him tremendous popular support when he left the Liberal Party a few years later and founded the Parti Québécois. Robert Bourassa rode the promise of James Bay into power in 1970 and again in 1972; his mishandling of the project led to cost overruns and labour strife among the construction workers at the dam sites and cost him the election of 1976. Jacques Parizeau became finance minister because of that election.

Even Brian Mulroney owes much of his political success to James Bay. It was as a lawyer on the much-publicized Cliche Commission which investigated corrupt practices in the construction work at James Bay that he first gained national prominence. He was able to parley this into a third-place finish at the 1976 Conservative leadership convention, and eventually into victory over Joe Clark in 1983. None of these leaders is likely to abandon the project to which their political careers have been tied almost from birth.

Pssst! Wanna Buy A $15 Billion Hydro Project?

To be fair, nobody seems to be saying they favour the outright seizure by Canada of the James Bay Project. David Bercuson and Barry Cooper suggest in their book that the same rules which were followed when Rupert's Land was transferred to Canada should serve as a precedent for the transfer of this territory back to federal jurisdiction:

> Concerning the assets currently in place in the former territory of Rupert's Land that owe their existence to action undertaken by the government of the Province of Quebec or by Quebec investors, the precedents established in the negotiations between the Hudson Bay Company, the Colonial Office, and Canada would apply. Canada and Quebec would, therefore, negotiate an "indemnification" package to compensate Quebec for such major capital projects as the James Bay hydroelectric developments and the iron-ore railway to Schefferville.[86]

In his book, *Who Gets Ungava?*, David Varty favours a similar solution, although he feels that compensation for James Bay should be tied to Quebec's compensation to Canada for federal assets in that portion of Quebec that he would permit to secede. He admits that French-speaking Quebecers might find this solution difficult to accept:

> There would probably be a divided response. Some Quebecers would advocate war to take the territory. Others would argue that it is not worth a civil war and that the main purpose of the separation from Canada is to protect the St. Lawrence based francophone culture.[87]

The thought that his proposals could start loose talk of war does not concern him greatly, although the reason for his self-confidence may be alarming to those of us who are more timid:

> Canada has a distinct advantage. Canadian military forces are under the control and direction of the Federal government. It is a power granted to Parliament by section 91(7) of the Constitution Act, 1867. The total armed forces strength in 1988 was 87,448. Canada has a military arsenal of tanks, aircraft and ships in place. The Republic of Quebec would be starting to build its military forces from scratch.[88]

Even if the Quebec government showed an unexpected willingness to sell the James Bay Project, nobody could afford to buy it. Certainly the Cree could not afford the multi-billion dollar pricetag. Neither could debt-ridden Canada. Ownership of the project implies possession of its liabilities as well as its assets, and this presumably means that Canada would be saddled with some of the very unfavourable long term contracts signed between Hydro-Québec and the companies that own aluminum and magnesium smelting plants along the banks of the St. Lawrence. Some of these contracts tie the price which the plants will pay for their power supply to the international price of the commodities they produce, and are so poorly drafted that when the price of aluminum or magnesium drops, Hydro-Québec is required to supply electricity at about half its cost of production. (The long term trend seems to be for the price of primary commodities like aluminum and magnesium to continue to drop.) In assuming ownership of the project, Canada would face not only a massive initial outlay of cash, but also a long-term subsidy of heavy industry in an independent Quebec.

Worse yet, Hydro-Québec is saddled with a long-term debt of $22 billion, or over $3,500 for every person in Quebec. Hydro-Québec's debts are so enormous that the utility is currently the world's largest corporate user of long-term U.S. dollar-dominated debt instruments.[89] Canadian ownership of some large percentage of Hydro-Québec's assets would necessitate the assumption by Canada of a large share of this debt, which is something that Canada can ill afford in its present economic circumstances. It would be far more sage to leave the burden of owning the James Bay Project to the Québécois, even in the unlikely event that they express a willingness to part with it.

Partitioning Baie-James Without a Fight

The only way to defuse the James Bay mess will be to find a solution that lets each side keep what it already has, and to grant each side sovereignty over its own assets and population in the region. This means that we will have to abandon the notion of neat, tidy blocks of sovereign territory, and resort to a more creative solution.

I recommend the adoption of a two-step partition formula for Baie-James township. In the first stage, voting results would be tabulated by polls. The result of this would be small islands of pro-Quebec territory and other islands of pro-Canada territory in a vast sea of unpartitioned land. (Baie-James is, along with Nunavik, one of only two municipalities in Quebec that are not fully divided into polls.)

In the second stage, all remaining land in Baie-James township would be awarded to the country to which the Crees vote to adhere. Beneficial use of the whole of this territory would be awarded to the Cree nation, which needs the land to support its rapidly growing population. Having exploded from 6,000 to 12,000 over the past two decades, the Cree population can only be kept from sliding into massive poverty and unemployment if it has access to the forms of employment for which the Natives have a comparative skill advantage: namely hunting, trapping, and fishing. These are land-intensive activities. In the barren north there is no other current economic use for the vast unflooded stretches of land between the dams and reservoirs than these nomadic hunter-gatherer practices.

All lands lying inside the polls which voted to remain part of Quebec would remain under the jurisdiction of Quebec law, as

would all lands containing real property and physical infrastructure necessary to the continued function of Phase I of the James Bay
Project. The question of nominal sovereignty over these lands is
complicated and will be dealt with below. In practice, the arrangement would have to include the following three concessions to
Quebec: the right of all francophones in the region to live under the
exclusive jurisdiction of Quebec laws and to travel to and from the
main territory of Quebec without leaving this jurisdiction (in essence, the same rights that I have advocated for Canadians passing
from Montreal to the Ontario border); the continued total control
of the hydro dams and levees of James Bay by the Quebec government; and unhindered access to all of the physical infrastructure of
the project, including all access roads and all of the hundreds of
miles of hydro lines. All private property rights, including the
Quebec government's right of proprietary ownership over all
Hydro-Québec property in the region, would have to be guaranteed.

These conditions could be met one of two ways. Quebec could
be granted a long-term lease over these lands, similar to the ninety-
nine-year lease which Britain gained over Hong Kong's Kowloon
Peninsula in 1898 or the permanent lease which the United States
awarded itself over Cuba's Guantanamo Bay in the wake of the
Spanish-American War. An even better parallel is the twenty-year
lease which the United States signed with Panama in 1977, giving
Panama nominal sovereignty over the Panama Canal Zone, effective as of 1979, but permitting the continued operation of United
States law in the Canal Zone until December 31, 1999.

As a more permanent alternative to a lease, Quebec could be
granted perpetual sovereignty over these areas. This would parallel the situation that existed in the Panama Canal Zone between
1904 and 1979, during which period the Canal Zone was as much
a part of the U.S., both in practice and law, as the many other
American exclaves that still exist today: Alaska, the Virgin Islands,
Guam, American Samoa, etc.

Both systems have worked well in Panama; the only practical
difference between them is the time limit on the present Canal
Zone lease. Applied to the territory of Baie-James township, either
one would produce a spider web-like pattern of territory over
which Quebec would have continued control. This would look odd
on a map, but no more odd than the Panama Canal Zone.

The Panama Canal Zone: An Example for Northern Quebec?

The circumstances surrounding the signing of the Panama Canal Zone Treaty of 1977 form an almost perfect parallel to the situation today in northern Quebec. The Canal Zone had been American soil only since 1904, while the part of Quebec where most of the James Bay infrastructure is located has been part of the province only since 1912. The canal itself was completed in 1914 with American money, and was the object of considerable national pride for the United States, just as James Bay is a source of immense pride for Quebec nationalists. The continued operation of the canal was a matter of importance for American national security. In the 1970s international Communism was still seen as a major threat; the Americans were concerned that if Panama aligned itself with the Soviet Bloc, U.S. warships would no longer be able to use the canal.

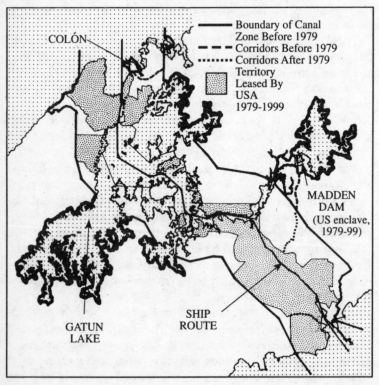

Panama Canal Zone. (Fig. 26)

These factors militated against the return of the Canal Zone to Panamanian sovereignty. In Quebec, the argument is for national economic security and the continuation of the annual $2 billion revenue flow from the project.

Another important argument against returning the Zone was the fact that the entire canal apparatus was operated by American citizens. In 1978, the Canal Zone had a population of 34,000 Americans. 'Zonians,' as American residents are known, are perhaps the most patriotic Americans anywhere. (They continue to this day to lead the United States in the number of Boy Scouts per capita, for example.) They had no wish to become Panamanians.

The 10,000 engineers, technicians, and others who provide the human infrastructure for the James Bay project are equally patriotic—towards the budding nation-state of Quebec. In the referendum of 1980, the region was one of the few in Quebec to record a strong 'Yes' vote for Sovereignty-Association. As in the Canal Zone, the local economy in the French-speaking towns of the James Bay region is entirely artificial. The giant hydroelectric project is the only reason why more than a handful of French Canadians live in the region. (In 1912, when the area containing the James Bay Project was awarded to Quebec, its population included fewer than a dozen francophones.)

Details of the Panama Canal Treaties

In 1977, the United States signed a treaty with the Republic of Panama under which the Americans gave up their permanent right to govern the Panama Canal Zone in exchange for a twenty-year lease over the Canal Zone's key operating installations. The Americans agreed to transfer sovereignty largely because they realized that the Canal Zone was militarily indefensible. A compromise with Panamanian nationalism was necessary if the United States was to avoid the danger of terrorist attacks against the canal's vulnerable infrastructure (another similarity to James Bay).

In return for their concessions, the Americans won stronger protection for their real interest in the canal, which is military. They were granted the permanent right to defend the canal, and the right to send warships through the canal whenever necessary. Approval of the Panama Canal Treaty was tied to ratification of another treaty guaranteeing the permanent neutrality of the canal. Similarly, Quebec's real interest in the James Bay region lies not in the abstract notion of sovereignty over a large chunk of territory inhabited by Natives who feel no loyalty to the Quebec state, but in the maintenance of a continued revenue stream from a $15 billion investment.

Effective upon the signing of the treaty, the United States surrendered control over most of the Canal Zone's territory to Panama. Control was retained over military installations and a narrow strip

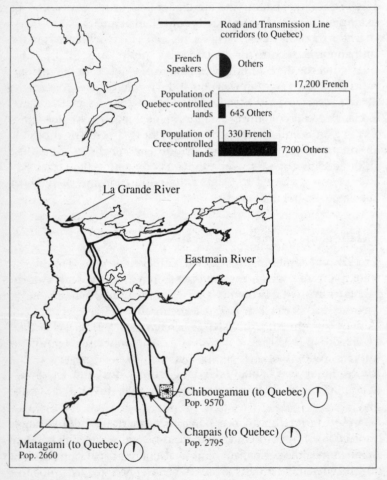

James Bay Region. (Fig. 27)

of territory on either side of the canal. Certain other key installations, such as the Madden Lake hydroelectric dam, which provides the electricity that powers the canal locks, were made into American enclaves. On these limited territories, American law continues to prevail, even though Panamanian sovereignty is recognized. They are essentially territories 'on lease.' In addition, the Americans have the right to travel unhindered on the roads connecting the various enclaves, and to maintain the hydro lines from Madden Dam as necessary, without interference. The broad body of Panamanian law applies to Americans going about their activities in these areas, but the Panamanians may not unduly hinder or regulate these tasks. For instance, Panamanian licensing laws do not apply in these corridors.

It is important to stress that, for comparative purposes, the valuable part of the Panama Canal Treaty model is not the relatively short twenty-year lease, but the technical details by which the United States continues to operate an enormous installation on the territory of another state. My opinion is that it would be impossible to convince the Quebec government to accede to anything less than a permanent lease of James Bay's hydroelectric installations. Given the fact that more francophones than Crees live in the region, this is not an unreasonable demand. Nor would it be impractical or unreasonable for Quebec to go further in its demands and insist upon retaining full sovereignty over these limited pieces of territory.

If the system used in the Canal Zone between 1904 and 1979 were followed exactly, the corridors containing the access roads and transmission lines would be no wider than the minimum necessary to permit their normal function. The details of the operation of these corridors were discussed in Chapter Six and do not need to be repeated here. Applied to Baie-James township, the corridor principle would require some simple modifications. The right of hunters to pursue migrating caribou across the corridors would have to be guaranteed. The width of the corridors used for transmitting electricity would have to be altered from the Panamanian model to reflect the special needs of long-distance electrical transmission lines. Adequate space for rest stations and emergency facilities would have to be included in the road corridors, due to the great distances involved.

The corridor solution is not as alien to the northern Quebec experience as one might at first imagine. Corridors already exist

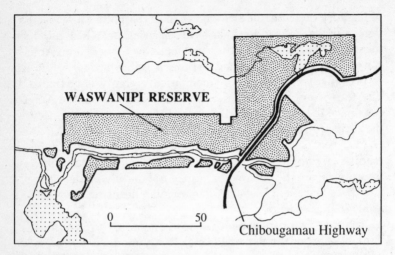

Waswanipi corridor. (Fig. 28)

along some of the access roads in the James Bay region. Where the
road running southwest from Chibougamau to Abitibi passes
through Waswanipi Reserve, a corridor of provincially-owned
land has been cut through the Reserve. The Crees of Waswanipi are
not prevented from using the road for their own purposes, but they
cannot obstruct the roadways or impose a toll for its use, as they
might if they owned the land. The proposal outlined above is really
just an extension of this model.

SUMMARY

The Natives of Quebec make no secret of their primary allegiance:
they are dedicated to the flowering of their own ancestral nations.
But if they have to choose between existing within Quebec or
Canada, it is likely that, in the aftermath of Oka, they would choose
Canada. It is important that policy-makers not forget the legitimate
interests of the Natives as they develop plans for partitioning
Quebec. Canadians must remember the following:

- **Major conflict must be avoided at all costs.**
  There exists a very real potential for major conflict between Quebec and Native interests. This must be avoided
  not only for its own sake, but also because it would

seriously complicate the procedure of establishing new borders between Canada and Quebec in all minority areas of the province.

- **Canada must legislate an impartial legal apparatus for mediating between the conflicting goals of Quebec and the aboriginal nations.**
  It will be legally impossible for Quebec to define its new boundaries as a state until it has negotiated comprehensive treaties with all its aboriginal nations. The treaty-making process must therefore be put on a fast track. The process must ensure a fair hearing for both aboriginal and Québécois aspirations.

- **Canada must take the leading role in arbitration.**
  If Quebec refuses to discuss partition with regard to its Native peoples, Canada must take the initiative and negotiate self-government treaties with the aboriginal nations of Quebec.

- **Make special arrangements for the Cree of James Bay.**
  A serious confrontation is brewing between the Cree and Hydro-Québec. Special arrangements must be made to accommodate the needs of both parties in this volatile situation.

Conclusion

I began this book asking you to 'imagine the unimaginable': Canada in the grip of armed conflict. This requires a mighty leap of imagination for most Canadians, who have come to view themselves as the most peaceful people on the globe. Like me, they were brought up to believe that Canada solves all its problems peaceably.

Perhaps this is because Canada is still a very young country. Unlike Yugoslavia, Ireland, and so many other parts of the world, English and French Canadians have not built up hundreds of years of injustices and unresolved vendettas. Canada, as Mackenzie King observed shortly after his return to power in the mid-1930s, is distinguished from the nations of Europe by the fact that it suffers from too much geography rather than a surfeit of history. A badly handled separation and partition crisis would solve Canada's geographical problem and its lack of history at the same time. My greatest fear is that Canada may abandon the search for peaceful solutions to the problems that will beset it in the future, and adopt the methods of old states. I fear that Canada, with or without Quebec, may grow old and bitter.

The crisis in Quebec today could be the beginning of truly negative relations between Quebec and Canada forever, if we are not careful. One need only contemplate the many proposals now being set forth in English Canada as final solutions to the partition of Quebec to see the roots of future conflict. It was reading these proposals that instilled in me my fear for Canada. This book is, in part, a response to their strong, proud, and thoroughly unreasonable words.

The question was, is, and likely will be: what do Canadians want? They want a land stretching from sea to sea, prosperous, clean and free. But they also want to be fair players, and this means respecting the right of provinces to leave Confederation. Canadians want it all. If or when Quebec leaves, Canadians will have to adjust to a new order and create new myths to replace the old, shattered ideals of federalist unity. They will have little or no choice in this. They will just have to do it.

Where Canada has choice is in what direction it wants the new order to take. Does it want to follow Yugoslavia? I do not believe so. But Canada must decide, and quickly, how it wishes to deal with the future. If it wishes to avoid creating a tradition of violence and intolerance, then it must create a legal, constitutional method for Quebec, or any province, to separate if it so chooses. The procedure should be entrenched in the Constitution. This would eliminate the danger of illegal action by either party in a separation crisis.

A tolerant and peaceful future requires the participation of everyone: Canadians, Quebecers, francophones, anglophones, and Natives. No group can be disqualified from the conversation of nationhood. To do so would compromise the democratic tradition of Canada.

APPENDIX A

Amendments to the Berne Constitution Concerning Jurassian Secession And Partition

1. GENERAL REGULATIONS CONCERNING REFERENDA

Article 1

There may, conforming to the regulations which follow, be organized referenda ["popular consultations"] in the Jurassian part of the canton, which includes the districts of Courtelary, Delémont, Franches-Montagnes, Laufen, Moutier, La Neuveville, and Porrentruy, which are mentioned in the Decree of 16 November 1939 on the division of the Canton of Berne into 30 districts. These referenda shall determine whether the entire Jurassian part of the canton or certain of its regions will form a new canton, attach themselves to another canton, or continue to be part of the Canton of Berne.

Article 2

1. A first referendum may be organized in the Jurassian part of the canton on the following question: "Do you want to create a new canton?"
2. This referendum will follow:
    a. at the request of 5,000 enfranchised citizens from the Jurassian part of the canton; or
    b. at the discretion of the Executive Council.

Article 3

1. If the first referendum produces a majority in favour of creating a new canton, but if one or more districts produce a majority rejecting this, it shall be possible in the six months following the referendum for a fifth of the electors in each of these districts to petition for a new referendum to be organized, on the question of whether that district will continue to be part of the Canton of Berne.
2. If the first public referendum does not produce a majority in favour of creating a new canton, but if one or more of the districts produces a majority in favour, it shall be possible in the six months following the referendum for a fifth of the electors in each of these districts to petition for a new referendum to be organized, on the question of whether the district should separate from the Canton of Berne.

Article 4

1. If the referenda which follow reveal, in one or more districts, a majority in favour of the creation of a new canton, a supplementary referendum can be demanded in the two months following by the communes that share a border with a district to which they wish to be annexed.
2. The supplementary referendum shall be limited to the question of whether the commune or communes will continue to be part of the Canton of Berne or will separate.
3. Referenda will be permitted if a fifth of the electors request it in the form of a communal initiative. The referendum will take place within two months following the deposit of the initiative.
4. Article 8 below applies to the right to vote and to participate in the communal initiative.

Article 5

If the separation procedure has begun, and if this procedure does not involve the district of Laufen, in the two years which follow a fifth of the electors in this district can petition for a referendum on the question of whether to annex themselves to a neighbouring canton.

Article 6

The periods mentioned in Article 3, Article 4 (paragraph 1), and Article 5 will begin on the day that they have been put into action as a result of a preceding referendum.

Article 7

1. If it is presented with requests for popular referendums under the terms of Articles 2, 3, and 5, the Grand Council shall determine whether they conform to the present regulations.
2. If this is the case, it will determine the exact date of the referenda, which may take place not less than three months, nor more than six months, after this decision has been made.
3. The referenda will not take place at the same time as any regularly-scheduled election.

Article 8

The right to petition for a referendum and the right to participate will be granted to citizens having the right to vote on cantonal matters and who:

    a. are domiciled in a commune in the region in which the referendum is requested; or
    b. are domiciled not less than three months in the region.

2. ENACTING THE LEGAL CONSEQUENCES OF THE REFERENDA

Article 9

The Grand Council shall take action within four months of the results of the referenda which may take place under Articles 2, 3, 4, and 5.

Article 10

The separation procedures for the entire Jurassian part of the canton will be introduced:

a. when the first referendum has furnished a majority in favour of the creation of a new canton; and

b. when the possibilities present under Article 3 have not been used within the allotted time, or have been used without success.

Article 11

1. The Grand Council will designate by decree the territory for which the separation procedure will be opened. Included within this territory will be:

a. those districts which decide in favour of separation, except for those communes which have decided, in referenda as described in Article 4, to be part of the Canton of Berne; and

b. those communes in neighbouring districts which have declared themselves in favour of separation by means of a referendum in the sense of Article 4.

2. The Grand Council hereby delimits the electoral regions which will be used for the election of a Constituent Assembly: these electoral regions will correspond to the districts with the modifications which result from the application of paragraph 1.

Article 12

If a new referendum is held in the District of Laufen, as described in Article 5, and if this referendum produces a majority in favour of annexation to another canton, this district will organize the necessary administration for the purpose of developing a procedure of separation and annexation. The details of the procedure of separation and annexation of the district of Laufen will be regulated by appropriate legislation.

3. ELECTION OF A CONSTITUENT ASSEMBLY

Article 13

1. When it has been established that the separation procedure has begun and when the territory which will participate in the separation has been determined, the Grand Council will establish a date for the election of a Constituent Assembly.

2. The election will take place not less than three months and not more than six months following the decision of the Grand Council.

Article 14

1. The Constituent Assembly for the whole of the Jurassian part of the canton will consist of 80 members.

2. The members of the Constituent Assembly will be elected in the districts of the Jurassian parts of the canton following the regulations applicable to the election of members of the Grand Council.

3. Each district will constitute an electoral region.

4. A decree of the Grand Council will divide the electoral regions according to the population therein domiciled as recorded in the latest federal census.

5. The Constituent Assembly will be elected for a period of six years. Re-election will be possible.

Article 15

1. The Constituent Assembly for the entire Jurassian part of the canton will consist of 50 members.

2. The members will be elected in the electoral regions regulated by the application of Article 11 (paragraph 2), and according to the regulations applicable to the election of members of the Grand Council.
3. Paragraphs 4 and 5 of Article 14 apply equally in this case as well.

Article 16

1. The Executive Council will open the first session of the Constituent Assembly on the fourth Monday following the day of the vote. In case of appeal against the election, the opening can be delayed until the closure of the investigation.
2. The Constituent Assembly will establish the power of its members and establish its own rules.

Article 17

1. The Constituent Assembly will develop a constitution for the new canton.
2. The constitution will be submitted to a vote by the electors of a new canton. The Constituent Assembly will determine the right to participate in this vote. If the constitution is rejected by the electorate, it will elect a new Constituent Assembly to develop a new constitution.

Article 18

If the citizens accept the constitution, the Executive Council will request a federal guarantee for it.

Article 19

Once the federal guarantee has been accorded to the constitution of the new canton, the Executive Council will request the modification of the first of Articles 1 and 80 of the federal constitution by use of the right of cantonal initiative.

Article 20

As limited by the present regulations, and by regulations which may be adopted by the federal authorities, the cantonal right of initiative applies to the request for the organization of a referendum, to the referendum itself, as well as to the procedures which follow.

Article 21

If the Federal Assembly grants a federal guarantee to these regulations, the Executive Council will approach the Federal Council to obtain from it the necessary measures to assure the orderly enactment of referenda, elections to a Constituent Assembly, and voting concerning the new constitution.

Article 22

1. The Executive Council will fix the date on which these regulations will enter into force.
2. It cannot take this decision until:
   a. the federal guarantee has been granted; and/or
   b. the Grand Council has passed regulations on the recommendations of the Executive Council regarding the status of Jura, which will include in particular regulations regarding the district of Laufen.

TABLE 1. FORMULA FOR DETERMINING WHICH POLLS WILL VOTE TO STAY IN CANADA

(assuming all francophones vote to join Quebec and all non-francophones vote to remain in Canada)

RIDING	Total Pop. of Riding[1]	Non-Franco-phone Pop. of Riding[2]	Total # of valid votes cast in Election of 1989	# of non-Franco-phone votes Cast	# of votes cast for Equality or Unity Party	% of non-franco-phone votes cast for EP/UP[3]
Argenteuil	49,090	9,417 (18%)	27,328	5,083	4,052	80%
Beauharnois-Huntingdon	47,210	9,994 (21%)	25,601	5,376	3,969	74%
Bonaventure	39,470	6,498 (16%)	19,744	3,258	1,266	39%
Brome-Mississquoi	47,445	14,312 (30%)	24,922	7,526	2,756	37%
Chateauguay	51,840	14,300 (28%)	28,707	7,923	5,007	63%
Chomedey	61,923	26,721 (43%)	31,642	13,606	5,889	43%
D'Arcy McGee	52,040	44,657 (86%)	27,219	23,408	15,746	67%
Deux-Montagnes	57,175	7,080 (12%)	33,681	4,143	2,449	59%
Gaspé	45,835	5,003 (10%)	22,131	2,412	1,160	48%
Gatineau	45,840	8,663 (19%)	21,750	4,133	2,446	59%
Groulx	58,550	6,960 (12%)	35,729	4,252	1,589	37%
Hull	58,720	7,658 (13%)	25,301	3,289	751	23%
Jacques-Cartier	62,655	46,539 (74%)	33,764	24,985	14,821	59%
Jeanne-Mance	61,320	25,330 (42%)	26,584	11,165	1,930	17%
Johnson	47,945	2,227 (5%)	25,863	1,190	401	34%
Laporte	53,630	17,486 (33%)	29,611	9,772	7,436	76%

RIDING	Total Pop. of Riding[1]	Non-Francophone Pop. of Riding[2]	Total # of valid votes cast in Election of 1989	# of non-Francophone votes Cast	# of votes cast for Equality or Unity Party	% of non-francophone votes cast for EP/UP[3]
Marguerite-Bourgeoys	52,240	27,299 (52%)	25,506	13,263	6,171	47%
Marquette	54,910	18,633 (34%)	27,532	9,361	4,762	51%
Megantic-Compton	39,915	3,601 (9%)	20,878	1,878	1,039	55%
Mont-Royal	53,040	34,968 (66%)	20,245	13,362	5,681	43%
Nelligan	62,895	33,794 (54%)	34,627	18,699	10,249	55%
Notre-Dame-de-Grace	56,510	42,982 (76%)	27,047	20,556	11,638	57%
Orford	55,415	8,010 (14%)	29,988	4,348	1,696	39%
Pontiac	47,865	22,045 (46%)	20,434	9,502	6,259	66%
Richmond	45,120	3,011 (7%)	24,108	1,615	506	31%
Robert Baldwin	59,210	3,9791 (67%)	27,515	18,435	11,287	61%
Sainte-Anne	47,970	15,101 (31%)	22,072	6,842	3,057	45%
St-François	55,470	5,944 (11%)	28,786	3,085	1,881	61%
Saint-Jean	62,545	4,370 (7%)	36,198	2,529	782	31%
Saint-Laurent	63,100	34,077 (54%)	29,720	16,049	7,101	44%
Saint-Louis	61,950	30,789 (50%)	22,260	11,063	3,815	34%
Shefford	60,280	4,004 (7%)	35,134	2,319	1,091	47%
Vaudreuil	53,420	13,205 (25%)	31,410	7,758	2,852	36%
Verdun	41,990	15,114 (36%)	21,503	7,741	4,857	63%
Viger	52,205	19,117 (27%)	27,741	7,490	1,831	24%
Westmount	47,350	33,365 (70%)	21,658	15,160	8,801	58%

NOTES TO TABLE ONE:

1. Total population and non-francophone population figures are derived from figures provided in the *Dossiers Socio-économiques* published by the Directeur Général des Elections, Quebec City, August 1989.

2. Total non-francophone population includes the following statistical groups: English mother tongue, non-official language mother tongue, persons with both English and non-official language as mother tongue, and half of all respondents who gave both English and French (or English, French and a third language) as mother tongue. The *Dossiers Socio-économiques* did not provide breakdowns of multiple responses for the following ridings: Chomedy, D'Arcy McGee, Gatineau, Jacques Cartier, Jeanne-Mance, Maguerite-Bourgeoys, Marquette, Mont-Royal, Nelligan, Notre-Dame-de-Grace, Robert-Baldwin, Ste-Anne, St- François, St-Laurent, St-Louis, Verdun, Viger, and Westmount. For these ridings I have divided up the total multiple responses proportionately to the linguistic breakdown of the single responses.

3. Any poll in which this percentage of the total vote was cast for the Unity/Equality Party Candidate is assumed to be 100% non-francophone. Any poll in which half this percentage of the vote was cast for the EP/UP candidate is assumed to be 50% non-francophone and therefore likely to vote to remain in Canada, if a poll-by-poll referendum is held.

TABLE 2. FORMULA FOR DETERMINING POPULATION AND ETHNIC MIX OF POLLS

	1. Total votes cast for E.P/ U.P candidate in polls awarded to Canada	2. Total valid ballots cast in polls awarded to Canada	3. Divide by fraction of non-francophones in the riding who cast votes for Equality/Unity	4. Multiply figure in column #1 by figure in column #3	5. Divide total population of riding by number of valid ballots cast in riding	6. Total pop. of polls awarded to Canada (#2 x #5)	7. Total non-francophone pop. of polls awarded to Canada (#4 x #5)	8. Total franco-phone pop. of polls awarded to Canada (#6 minus #7)
Argenteuil	1,126	2,269	1/.797=1.255	1,413	1.796	4,075	2,538	1,537
Beauharnois-Huntingdon	1,917	3,997	1/.740=1.351	2,590	1.844	7,370	4,776	2,594
Bonaventure	683	1,957	1/.390=2.564	1,751	1.999	3,912	3,500	412
Brome-Mississquoi	1,087	4,404	1/.367=2.725	2,962	1.904	8,385	5,640	2,745
Chateauguay	1,775	4,089	1/.632=1.582	2,808	1.806	7,385	5,071	2,314
Chomedey	4,032	11,022	1/.433=2.309	9,309	1.957	21,570	18,218	3,352
D'Arcy McGee	15,746	27,219	1/.673=1.486	23,399	1.912	52,042	44,739	7,303
Gaspé	371	982	1/.480=2.083	773	2.071	2,034	1,601	432
Gatineau	1,390	2,792	1/.590=1.695	2,356	2.107	5,883	4,964	919
Groulx	300	1,485	1/.370=2.703	810	1.639	2,434	1,328	1,106
Hull	0	0					0	0
Jacques-Cartier	13,636	29,803	1/.593=1.686	22,990	1.856	55,314	42,669	12,645
Jeanne-Mance	991	8,677	1/.172=5.814	5,762	2.307	20,018	13,293	6,724
Johnson	148	624	1/.337=2.967	439	1.854	11,569	814	343
Marguerette-Bourgeoys	4,633	16,456	1/.465=2.151	9,966	2.048	33702	20,410	13,292
Marquette	2,682	7,810	1/.509=1.965	5,270	1.994	15,573	10,508	5,065
Megantic-Compton	564	1,487	1/.553=1.808	1,020	1.912	2,843	1,950	893
Mont-Royal	4,614	12,626	1/.425=2.353	10,864	2.620	33,159	28,464	4,694
Nelligan	7,982	20,236	1/.548=1.825	14,567	1.816	36,749	26,454	10,295
Notre-Dame-de-Grace	10,792	23,186	1/.566=1.767	19,069	2.089	48,436	39,835	8,601
Orford	758	2,856	1/.390=2.564	1,944	1.848	5,278	3,593	1,683
Pontiac	3,515	7,625	1/.659=1.517	5,332	2.342	17,858	12,488	5,370
Richmond	82	313	1/.310=3.226	265	1.872	585	469	89
Robert Baldwin	10,904	25,623	1/.610=1.639	17,872	2.152	55,141	38,461	16,680

	1. Total votes cast for E.P/ U.P candidate in polls awarded to Canada	2. Total valid ballots cast in polls awarded to Canada	3. Divide by fraction of non-francophones in the riding who cast votes for Equality/Unity	4. Multiply figure in column # 1 by figure in column #3	5. Divide total population of riding by number of valid ballots cast in riding	6. Total pop. of polls awarded to Canada (#2 x #5)	7. Total non-francophone pop. of polls awarded to Canada (#4 x #5)	8. Total franco-phone pop. of polls awarded to Canada (#6 minus #7)
Sainte-Anne	829	2,902	1/.446=2.242	1,859	2.173	6,306	4,040	2,266
St-Francois	887	2,061	1/.609=1.642	1,456	1.927	3,972	2,806	1,166
Saint-Jean	87	398	1/.309=3.236	282	1.728	688	487	201
Saint-Laurent	5,208	14,224	1/.442=2.262	11,780	2.123	39,585	25,009	14,576
Saint-Louis	2,837	9,043	1/.344=2.907	8,247	2.783	25,167	22,951	2,213
Shefford	0	0				0	0	0
Vaudreuil	1,236	4,874	1/.360=2.778	3,433	1.701	8,291	5,840	2,451
Verdun	1,279	3,719	1/.627=1.595	2,040	1.953	7,263	3,984	3,279
Viger	304	2,221	1/.244=4.098	1,246	1.882	4,179	2,345	1,835
Westmount	7,870	17,282	1/.581=1.722	13,552	2.186	37,778	29,625	8,153

TABLE 3. FORMULA FOR DETERMINING POPULATION AND ETHNIC MIX OF ENCLAVES

(assuming all francophones vote to join Quebec and all non-francophones vote to remain in Canada)

MONTREAL

I. Main Canadian enclave on the Island of Montreal (to be retained by Canada):

Includes parts of the following ridings:

	1. Total votes cast for E.P./U.P candidate in enclave	2. Total valid ballots cast in enclave	3. Divide 1 by fraction of non-francophones in the riding who cast votes for Equality/Unity	4. Multiply figure in column 1 by figure in column #3	5. Divide total population of riding by number of valid ballots cast in riding	6. Total pop. of polls awarded to Canada (#2 x #5)	7. Total non-francophone pop. of polls awarded to Canada (#4 x #5)	8. Total francophone pop. of polls awarded to Canada (#6 minus #7)
D'Arcy McGee	15,746	27,219	1/.673=1.486	23,399	1.912	52,042	44,739	7,303
Jacques Cartier	13,636	29,803	1/.593=1.686	22,990	1.856	55,314	42,669	12,645
Marg. Bourgeoys	3,267	12,001	1/.465=2.151	7,028	2.048	24,578	14,393	10,185
Marquette	2,467	12,001	1/.509=1.965	4,848	1.994	14,207	9,666	4,541
Mont-Royal	4,614	12,626	1/.425=2.353	10,864	2.620	33,159	28,465	4,694
Nelligan	7,982	20,236	1/.548=1.825	14,567	1.816	36,749	26,454	10,295
N.D.G.	10,792	23,186	1/.566=1.767	19,069	2.089	48,436	39,835	8,601
Robert Baldwin	10,904	25,623	1/.610=1.639	17,872	2.152	55,141	38,461	16,680
St-Laurent	5,208	14,224	1/.442=2.262	11,780	2.123	39,585	25,009	14,576
St-Louis	2,837	9,043	1/.344=2.907	8,247	2.783	25,167	22,951	2,216
Westmount	7,870	17,282	1/.581=1.722	13,552	2.186	37,778	29,625	8,153

Laurier, Acadie and Outremont (No Equality Party candidates were run in these ridings, so these figures are estimates based upon Statistics Canada figures for census sub-districts):

TOTAL (this enclave): 422,156 | 322,267 | 99889

II. Other Canadian enclaves on the Island of Montreal (to be turned over to Quebec):

#1 (Includes parts of the following ridings):

	1.	2.	3.	4.	5.	6.	7.	8.
Viger	352	2,210	1/.581=4.098	1,442	1.882	4,159	2,714	1,445
Jeanne Mance	991	8,677	1/.172=5.814	5,762	2.307	20,018	13,293	6,725
TOTAL (this enclave):						24,177	16,007	8,170

	1. Total votes cast for E.P/ U.P candidate in enclave	2. Total valid ballots cast in enclave	3. Divide 1 by fraction of non-francophones in the riding who cast votes for Equality/Unity	4. Multiply figure in column #1 by figure in column #3	5. Divide total population of riding by number of valid ballots cast in riding	6. Total pop. of polls awarded to Canada (#2 x #5)	7. Total non-francophone pop. of polls awarded to Canada (#4 x #5)	8. Total franco-phone pop. of polls awarded to Canada (#6 minus #7)
#2 (Includes parts of the following ridings):								
St. Louis	127	671	1/.344=2.907	369	2.783	1,867	1,027	840
				TOTAL (this enclave):				
#3 (Includes parts of the following riding):								
Ste-Anne	826	2,619	1/.446=2.242	1,852	2.173	5,691	4,024	1,667
				TOTAL (this enclave):				
#4 (Includes parts of the following ridings):								
Marg. Bourgeoys	1,366	4,455	1/.465=2.151	2,938	2.048	9,124	6017	3107
Verdun	1,279	3,719	1/.627=1.595	2,040	1.953	7,263	3984	3279
				TOTAL (this enclave):		16,387	10,001	6,386

III. Enclave on Laval Island (to be retained by Canada):

#1. Includes part of Chomedey riding, in the city of Laval:

	1	2	3	4	5	6	7	8
	4032	11022	1/.433=2.309	9310	1.957	21,570	18,217	3353
				TOTAL (this enclave):				

IV. Quebec enclaves on the Island of Montreal (to be turned over to Canada):

	1	2	3	4	5	6	7	8
#1 (Includes parts of the following riding):								
Jacques Cartier	1185	3961	1/.593=1.686	1998	1.856	7352	3708	3644
				TOTAL (this enclave):				
#2 (Includes parts of the following riding):								
Nelligan	171	552	1/.548=1.825	312	1.816	948	567	381
				TOTAL (this enclave):				
#3 (Includes parts of the following riding):								
Mt. Royal	72	485	1/.425=2.353	169	2.620	1,271	443	828
				TOTAL (this enclave):				
#4 (Includes parts of the following ridings):								
N.D.G.	846	3,862	1/.556=1.767	1,495	2.089	8,068	3,123	4,945
Westmount	371	1,596	1/.581=1.722	639	2.186	3,489	1,397	2,092
				TOTAL (this enclave):		11,557	4,520	7,037

	1. Total votes cast for E.P/U.P candidate in enclave	2. Total valid ballots cast in enclave	3. Divide 1 by fraction of non-francophones in the riding who cast votes for Equality/Unity	4. Multiply figure in column #1 by figure in column #3	5. Divide total population of riding by number of valid ballots cast in riding	6. Total pop. of polls awarded to Canada (#2 x #5)	7. Total non-francophone pop. of polls awarded to Canada (#4 x #5)	8. Total francophone pop. of polls awarded to Canada (#6 minus #7)
#5 (Includes parts of the following riding): Westmount	31	146	1/.581=1.722	53 TOTAL (this enclave):	2.186	319	116	203
#6 (Includes parts of the following riding): Marg. Bourgeoys	376	1,894	1/.465=2.151	809 TOTAL (this enclave):	2.048	3,879	1,657	2,222
#7 (Includes parts of the following riding): Robert-Baldwin	176	883	1/.610=1.639	289 TOTAL (this enclave):	2.152	1,900	622	1,278
#8 (Includes parts of the following riding): Marquette	40	186	1/.509=1.965	79 TOTAL (this enclave) :	1.994	371	158	213

GASPE

Canadian Enclaves (to be turned over to Quebec):

#1 (Includes part of Gaspé township, in Gaspé riding):	107	238	1/.480=2.083	223 TOTAL (this enclave):	2.071	493	462	31
#2 (Includes parts of Gaspé & Percé townships, in Gaspé riding):	225	581	1/.480=2.564	469 TOTAL (this enclave):	2.071	1,203	971	232
#3 (Includes parts of Port-Daniel-partie-ouest and Shigawake townships, in Bonaventure riding):	183	346	1/.390=2.564	469 TOTAL (this enclave):	1.999	692	398	294
#4 (Includes the entire town of Hopetown, and part of the town of Hope, in Bonaventure riding):	112	371	1/.390=2.564	287 TOTAL (this enclave):	1.999	742	573	169

1. Total votes cast for E.P/U.P candidate in enclave	2. Total valid ballots cast in enclave	3. Divide 1 by fraction of non-francophones in the riding who cast votes for Equality/Unity	4. Multiply figure in column #1 by figure in column #3	5. Divide total population of riding by number of valid ballots cast in riding	6. Total pop. of polls awarded to Canada (#2 x #5)	7. Total non-francophone pop. of polls awarded to Canada (#4 x #5)	8. Total franco-phone pop. of polls awarded to Canada (#6 minus #7)
#5 (Includes part of the town of New Carlisle, in Bonaventure riding)							
226	633	1/.390=2.564	579	1.999	1,265	1,157	108
			TOTAL (this enclave):				108
#6 (Includes part of the town of New Richmond, in Bonaventure riding)							
73	406	1/.390=2.564	79	1.999	270	158	112
			TOTAL (this enclave):				112
#7 (Includes the town of Grande-Cascapédia and the Indian Reserve of Maria, as well as part of the town of St-Jules, in Bonaventure riding)							
85	241	1/.390=2.564	218	1.999	482	436	46
			TOTAL (this enclave):				46
#8 (Includes part of the town of Escuminac, in Bonaventure riding)							
46	166	1/.390=2.564	118	1.999	332	236	96
			TOTAL (this enclave):				96

EASTERN TOWNSHIPS

I. Canadian Exclaves (to be retained by Canada)

#1 (Includes parts of the following municipalities):

Havelock and Hemmingford townships, in Beauharnois-Huntingdon riding							
308	689	1.351	416	1.844	1271	767	504
Saint-Bernard-de-Lacombe township, in St-Jean riding							
44	150	3.236	142	1.728	259	245	14
			TOTAL (this exclave):		1,530	1,012	518

#2 (Includes parts of the following municipalities):

Saint-Armand-Ouest, Bedford, Stanbridge, Dunham, Sutton (ct), Sutton (v), Brome, Lake Brome, Brigham, East Farnham, West Bolton, and East Bolton, in Brome-Missisquoi riding

1,159	4,265	2.725	3,158	1.904	8,121	6,013	2,108
			TOTAL (this exclave):	1.904			2,108

	1. Total votes cast for E.P/U.P Candidate in enclave	2. Total valid ballots cast in enclave	3. Divide 1 by fraction of non-francophones in the riding who cast votes for Equality/Unity	4. Multiply figure in column #1 by figure in column #3	5. Divide total population of riding by number of valid ballots cast in riding	6. Total pop. of polls awarded to Canada (#2 x #5)	7. Total non-francophone pop. of polls awarded to Canada (#4 x #5)	8. Total franco-phone pop. of polls awarded to Canada (#6 minus #7)
#3 (Includes the entire territory of Abercom township, in Brome-Missisquoi riding):								
	36	157	2.725	98	1.904	298	186	112
TOTAL (this exclave):								**112**
#4 (Includes part of the territory of Potton township, in Brome-Missisquoi riding):								
	12	54	2.725	33	1.904	102	62	40
TOTAL (this exclave):								**40**
#5 (Includes parts of the following municipalities):								
Potton township, in Brome-Missisquoi riding								
	22	106	2.725	60	1.904	202	114	88
Stanstead, Stanstead East, Ogden, Beebe Plain, Rock Island, Ayer's Cliff, Hatley, Hatley-Partie-Ouest, North Hatley, in Orford riding								
	758	2,856	2.564	1,944	1.848	5,278	3,593	1,685
Lennoxville, Ascot, Waterville, Compton, and Compton Station, in St-Francois riding								
	887	2,061	1.642	1,457	1.927	3,972	2,808	1,164
TOTAL (this exclave):						**9,452**	**6,515**	**2,937**

II. Canadian Enclaves (to be turned over to Quebec)

	1.	2.	3.	4.	5.	6.	7.	8.
#1 (Includes part of the township of Tres-St-Sacrament, in Beauharnois-Huntington riding):								
	210	506	1.351	284	1.844	933	523	410
TOTAL (this enclave):								**410**
#3 (Includes all of Bury and Sawyerville townships and parts of Newport and Eaton townships, in Megantic-Compton riding):								
	564	1487	1.808	1020	1.912	2,843	1,950	893
TOTAL (this enclave):								**893**
#4 (Includes parts of the following municipalities):								
Melbourne (vl) and Melbourne (ct), in Johnson riding								
	140	624	2.967	415	1.854	1,157	769	388
Cleveland, in Richmond riding								
	82	313	3.226	265	1.872	586	496	90
TOTAL (this enclave):						**1,743**	**1,265**	**478**

	1. Total votes cast for E.P/U.P candidate in enclave	2. Total valid ballots cast in enclave	3. Divide 1 by fraction of non-francophones in the riding who cast votes for Equality/Unity	4. Multiply figure in column #1 by figure in column #3	5. Divide total population of riding by number of valid ballots cast in riding	6. Total pop. of polls awarded to Canada (#2 x #5)	7. Total non-francophone pop. of polls awarded to Canada (#4 x #5)	8. Total franco-phone pop. of polls awarded to Canada (#6 minus #7)

II. Quebec Exclaves (to be retained by Quebec)

#1 (Includes part of the township of Beebe Plain, in Orford riding):

	53	432	2.564	136	1.848	798	251	547
TOTAL (this exclave):								

WEST QUEBEC

I. Canadian Enclave on the route of the Montreal Road corridor (to be retained by Canada)

#1 Includes the town of Hudson, and parts of the townships of Vaudreuil, St-Lazare, and Ste-Madeleine-de-Rigaud, in Vaudreuil riding

	949	3,659	2.778	2,636	1.701	6,224	4,484	1,740
TOTAL (this enclave):								

II. Canadian Enclaves (to be turned over to Quebec)

#1 (Includes the township of Wentworth, and parts of the townships of Gore and Mille-Iles, in Argenteuil riding):

	305	636	1.255	383	1.796	1,142	688	454
TOTAL (this enclave):								

#2 (Includes part of the township of Morin Heights, in Argenteuil riding):

	7	110	1.255	59	1.796	198	106	92
TOTAL (this enclaver):								

#3 (Includes the township of Harrington and part of the township of Granville, in Argenteuil riding):

	378	645	1.255	474	1.796	1,158	851	307
TOTAL (this enclave):								

#4 (Includes part of the city of Aylmer, in Pontiac riding):

	585	1,611	1.517	887	2.342	3,738	2,078	1,695
TOTAL (this enclave):								

1. Total votes cast for E.P/ U.P candidate in enclave	2. Total valid ballots cast in enclave	3. Divide 1 by fraction of non-francophones in the riding who cast votes for Equality/Unity	4. Multiply figure in column #1 by figure in column #3	5. Divide total population of riding by number of valid ballots cast in riding	6. Total pop. of polls awarded to Canada (#2 x #5)	7. Total non-francophone pop. of polls awarded to Canada (#4 x #5)	8. Total francophone pop. of polls awarded to Canada (#6 minus #7)

III. Quebec Enclaves (to be turned over to Canada)

#1 (Includes part of Pontiac township, in Pontiac riding):

1.	2.	3.	4.	5.	6.	7.	8.
59	370	1.517	90	2.342	867	211	656
			TOTAL (this enclave):				

#2 (Includes parts of the following municipalities):

Pontiac township, in Pontiac riding

1.	2.	3.	4.	5.	6.	7.	8.
7	45	1.517	11	2.342	105	26	79

La Peche township, in Gatineau riding

1.	2.	3.	4.	5.	6.	7.	8.
74	1,095	1.645	125	2.107	2,307	263	2,044
			TOTAL (this enclave):		2,412	289	2,123

#3 (Includes part of Grand-Calumet township, in Pontiac riding):

1.	2.	3.	4.	5.	6.	7.	8.
28	254	1.517	42	2.342	595	98	497
			TOTAL (this enclave):				

#4 (Includes part of Ile-aux-Allumettes township, in Pontiac riding):

1.	2.	3.	4.	5.	6.	7.	8.
29	252	1.517	44	2.342	590	103	487
			TOTAL (this enclave):				

Footnotes

1. Marie-Josée Drouin and Brian Bruce-Biggs, *Canada Has a Future*. Toronto: McClelland and Stewart, 1978, p. 229.
2. Richard French, in Richard Simeon and Mary Janigan, editors, *Toolkits and Building Blocks: Constructing a New Canada*. Toronto: C.D. Howe Institute, 1991, p. 177.
3. Brian Mulroney is quoted in "Q & A: Brian Mulroney," in *Maclean's*. 2 January, 1992, p. 69.
4. Poll results reported in Montreal *Gazette*. 7 June, 1991, p. A8.
5. Percentage of Electorate Voting "Yes" (In favour of the Jurassian nationalist position):

	First Round (1974)		Third Round (1975)	
	Towns voting YES	Towns voting NO	Towns voting YES	Towns voting NO
Chatillon	87		90	
Corban	93		97	
Courchapoix	97		100	
Courrendlin	62		61	
Les Genevez	91		97	
Grandval		35		1
Lajoux	90		96	
Mervelier	85		93	
Moutier		49		46
Perrefitte		40		1
Rebévelier		24		9
Roggenburg		35		17
Rossemaison	84		97	
AVERAGE	86.1	36.6	91.4	14.8
PERCENT DIFF:	49.5		76.6	

Figures are from vote totals in the Jura Referendum of June 23, 1974 and the local plebiscites of September 7 and 14 and October 19, 1975, as compiled in John Jenkins, *Jura Separatism in Switzerland* (Oxford, Clarendon Press, 1986, Appendix C: Table 2). (For this exercise I counted the percent votes only in those towns which participated in the third round of voting in Autumn 1975; most communities in the Jura were prohibited from doing so by law or else chose not to participate. For the purposes of the calculation involved in the exercise, I divided the towns into two groups according to the direction of the vote in the final round of balloting, assigned an equal weight to the total in each community, regardless of the size of its voting population, and added up the results. —S.R.)

6. Population figures for Northern Ireland from *Ulster Year Book*, 1950. Belfast: His Majesty's Stationery Office, 1951, p. 41.

7. Article XII of the Anglo-Irish Treaty of 1921, quoted in Geoffrey Hand, editor, *Report of the Irish Boundary Commission*. Shannon, Ireland: 1969, p. 25.

8. *Ibid*. p. 52.

9. *Ibid*. pp. 47-48.

10. Population figures from map supplement to *Ibid*.

11. Quoted in Geoffrey Hand, Introduction to *Ibid*. p. xx.

12. The official documentation for the region is not as accurate as it is for other parts of Europe or for Canada. The Communist government of Josip Tito distorted census figures for the sake of maintaining Yugoslavia's delicate ethnic balance of power. The Yugoslav figures cited here should be taken as guides only.

13. Chuck Sudetic, "Croatia Endorses Independence Referendum," in *The Globe and Mail*. 20 May, 1991, p. 1.

14. Alan Ferguson, "Croatian Territorial Concessions Rejected," in Toronto *Star*. 19 August, 1991, p. 14.

15. Henri Brun maintains that Quebec owns roughly one-quarter of federal assets, based upon its share of the Canadian population. He considers this to include one-quarter of the landmass of the Yukon and the Northwest Territories. See Henri Brun, "Quebec Will Remain Intact If It Chooses to Separate," in *The Financial Post*, 17 February, 1992, p. S4; David Varty, "A Separate Quebec Will Lose Northern Territories," in *The Financial Post*, 17 February, 1992, p. S4.

16. See Article 2.1 of the section of the Constitution of the canton of Berne which deals with Jurassian separation. This section is reproduced in full as Appendix "A."

17. Députation du Jura bernois et de Bienne romande, *Réquête de la Députation du Jura bernois et de Bienne romande aux Chambres fédérales concernant la Constitution du futur canton du Jura et plus particulièrement son article 138*. Tramelan and Recônvilier, Berne: 12 May, 1977, p. 15.

18. Kenneth McRae, *Conflict and Compromise in Multilingual Societies: Switzerland*. Waterloo, Ontario: Wilfrid Laurier University Press, 1983, p. 193.

19. Landry is quoted in Sarah Scott, "What Would the 'New Quebec' Look Like?" in Montreal *Gazette*. 2 February, 1991, p. B1.

20. Jacques Brossard, *L'accession à la souveraineté et le cas du Québec*. Montreal: Les presses de l'université de Montréal, 1976, pp. 171-172.

21. *Ibid.* p. 173.
22. *Ibid.* p. xxx.
23. *Ibid.* p. 362.
24. *Ibid.* pp. 187, 490-492.
25. Lionel Albert and William Shaw, *Partition: The Price of Quebec's Independence.* Montreal: Thornhill, 1980, p. 135.
26. Kenneth McDonald, *Keeping Canada Together.* Toronto: Ramsey Business Systems, 1990, p. 40.
27. David Jay Bercuson and Barry Cooper, *Deconfederation: Canada Without Quebec.* Toronto: Key Porter, 1991, p. 157. (Italics are mine. —S.R.)
28. *Ibid.* p. 144.
29. *Ibid.* p. 156.
30. Ian Ross Robertson, "The Atlantic Provinces and the Territorial Question," in J.L. Granatstein and Kenneth McNaught, editors, *English Canada Speaks Out.* Toronto: Doubleday, 1991, p. 169.
31. *Ibid.* p. 170.
32. D.K. Donnelly, *Canamerican Union Now!* Toronto: Griffin House, 1978, p. 29.
33. Rod Manchee, letter to the editor, *Saturday Night.* September 1991, p. 8.
34. Albert and Shaw, *Partition.* p. 66.
35. *Ibid.* p. 71.
36. David Varty, *Who Gets Ungava?* Vancouver: Varty and Company, 1991, p. 31.
37. Albert and Shaw, *Partition: The Price of Quebec's Independence,* p. 79. Original citation is from a letter dated 19 September, 1763.
38. *Ibid.* p. 51.
39. Gaétan Lefebvre, letter to the editor, *Maclean's.* 9 December, 1991.
40. Lionel Albert, "Grappling with New Geography," in Ottawa *Citizen.* 4 April, 1991, p. A3.
41. Bercuson and Cooper, *Deconfederation.* p. 154.
42. René Lévesque, "For an Independent Quebec," in *Foreign Affairs.* July 1976, p. 741.
43. Brossard, *L'accession à la souveraineté.* p. 517.
44. All references to GATT are drawn from H.J. Lawford, "Treaties and Rights of Transit on the Saint Lawrence," *Canadian Bar Review.* 1961, p. 597.
45. Treaty of Washington, 1871, Article 26. Cited in Brossard, *L'accesion à la souveraineté.* p. 511.
46. Exchange of notes (August 17, 1954) between Canada and the United States of America, modifying the exchange of notes of June 30, 1952, concerning the construction of the St. Lawrence Seaway. Cited in *Ibid.* p. 588.
47. Peter C. Newman, "A Yes to Quebec From Mid-Canada," in *Maclean's.* 16 December, 1991, p. 29.
48. Pierre Berton, *Klondike.* Toronto: McClelland and Stewart, 1972, p. 218.
49. Bercuson and Cooper, *Deconfederation.* p. 154.
50. Arthur Phillips, *The Beachhead Principle.* Toronto: Simon and Pierre, 1977.

51. Bercuson and Cooper, *Deconfederation*. p. 162.
52. James Arnett in Simeon and Janigan, *Toolkits and Building Blocks*. p. 176.
53. Varty, *Who Gets Ungava?* p. 38. (Italics are mine. —S.R.)
54. Bercuson and Cooper, *Deconfederation*. p. 143.
55. Interviewed in Knowlton Nash, *Visions of Canada*. Toronto: McClelland and Stewart, 1991, p. 213.
56. Figure cited from 1986 census results as reported in *Canada Year Book*, 1990, p. 2-29.
57. To do this, I have taken the results from the 1980 referendum and assumed that the 'Yes' vote in each provincial electoral district would be 27 percent higher than it was in 1980. This would produce a 51 percent province-wide majority in favour of independence—just enough to justify a unilateral declaration of independence. I have awarded all districts with majorities in favour of independence to Quebec, and all others to Canada. (I would have preferred an arrangement based upon individual polls, but this is difficult to calculate and even harder to show on a large-scale map.)
58. Brossard, *L'accession à la souveraineté*. p. 358.
59. See the interview of Allan Blakeney in Knowlton Nash, *Visions of Canada*, p. 32.
60. All population and election statistics for the Jura are from the 1970 census figures cited in John Jenkins, *Jura Separatism in Switzerland*. Oxford: Clarendon Press, 1986, Appendix C, Table 1.
61. Figures from *Canada Year Book* 1990. pp. 17-19.
62. Brossard, *L'accession à la souveraineté*, p. 363. (Translation by Scott Reid. Italics in the original.)
63. The figures for poll populations and the ethnic breakdown of individual polls have been obtained by use of a formula based upon the votes gained by Equality Party and Unity Party candidates in the last provincial election. For the purposes of this formula it is assumed that all votes for these candidates were cast by non-francophones (this is not strictly correct, but is close to the truth). The formula is shown in tabular form in Appendix B.
64. See tables 1, 2, and 3 in Appendix B.
65. Ottawa *Citizen*, March 30, 1991, p. A5.
66. Details of the operation of the corridors may be found in a variety of treaties and conventions signed between 1904 and 1977. The clearest descriptions are contained in the *Convention Regarding the Colón Corridor and Certain Other Corridors*, signed in 1950. See especially Article III of this convention.
67. Philip Resnick, *Toward a Canada-Quebec Union*. Montreal and Kingston: McGill-Queen's University Press, 1991, p. 58.
68. See Drouin and Bruce-Biggs, *Canada Has a Future*. p. 17.
69. Societé d'aménagement de l'Outaouais, *Mémoire pour la Commission sur L'avenir Politique et Constitutionnel du Québec*. November 1990, p. 7. (Translation by Scott Reid.)
70. National Film Board of Canada, *Between Friends/Entre Amis*. Toronto: McClelland and Stewart, 1976.
71. The town also contains several exclaves of territory which adjoin the

main territory of the Kingdom of Belgium but do not touch each other. See Louis Malvoz, "Baerle-Duc et Baerle-Nassau: Trente-quatre Territoires pour Deux Communes," in *Crédit Communal de Belgique, Bulletin Trimestriel*, #155, January 1986, for a detailed history of this fascinating town.

72. Konrad Sioui is quoted in Richard Fidler (editor and translator), *Canada, Adieu? Quebec Debates its Future*. Lantzville, British Columbia and Halifax: Oolichan Books and The Institute for Research on Public Policy, 1991, p. 187.

73. Fiddler, ed. *Canada Adieu?* p. 183-184..

74. Brossard, *L'Accession à la souveraineté*. p. 187.

75. Cited in Fidler, ed., *Canada Adieu?* p. 181.

76. *Ibid.* p. 202.

77. Jacques Parizeau made this comment in the course of an interview with Dalton Camp. See Dalton Camp, "The Plot to Kill Canada," in *Saturday Night*. June 1991, p. 61.

78. Charlie Watt is quoted in Fidler, ed., *Canada, Adieu?* p. 199.

79. Billy Diamond is quoted in Maude Barlow and Bruce Campbell, *Take Back the Nation*. Toronto: Key Porter Books, 1991, p. 156.

80. Ted Moses is quoted in André Picard, "Cree Vow To Seize Land If Quebec Separates," in *The Globe and Mail*. 31 July, 1991, p. A1.

81. William Watson, "Quebec Separatists Ignore Logic," *The Financial Post*. 9 August, 1991, p. 9.

82. Matthew Coone-Come is quoted in Picard, "Cree Vow To Seize Land If Quebec Separates," in *The Globe and Mail*. 31 July, 1991, p. A2.

83. *Ibid.*

84. Conrad Black, *Duplessis*. Toronto: McClelland and Stewart, 1977, p. 692.

85. 46.2% in 1989. Figures are from Hydro-Québec, *Annual Report 1989*. Montreal: Hydro-Québec, 1990.

86. Bercuson and Cooper, *Deconfederation*. p. 152.

87. Varty, *Who Gets Ungava?* p. 61.

88. *Ibid.*

89. Robert Blohm, "Quebec Leads the Way in Foreign Borrowing," in *The Financial Post*. 8 March, 1991, p. 10.

Map Notes

Fig. 1   *Source:* Geoffrey Hand (ed.), *Report of the Irish Boundary Commission.* Shannon, Ireland, 1969.

Fig. 2   *Sources:* Francis Eterovich and Christopher Spalatin, *Croatia: Land, People, Culture.* Toronto: University of Toronto Press, 1970; Stephen Gazi, *A History of Croatia.* New York: Philosophical Library, 1973.

Fig. 4   *Sources:* Robert Domeniconi, *Le Canton du Jura: Statistiques Graphiques 1970-1975.* Delémont, Switzerland: Service d'Information de l'Assemblée contituante, 1978; John Jenkins, *Jura Separatism in Switzerland.* Oxford: Clarendon Press, 1986.

Fig. 5   *Sources:* Robert Domeniconi, *Le Canton du Jura: Statistiques Graphiques 1970-1975.* Delémont, Switzerland: Service d'Information de l'Assemblée contituante, 1978; John Jenkins, *Jura Separatism in Switzerland.* Oxford: Clarendon Press, 1986.

Fig. 6   *Sources:* Lionel Albert and William Shaw, *Partition: The Price of Quebec's Independence.* Montreal: Thornhill, 1980; Canada. Statistics Canada, *Population and Dwelling Characteristics—Census Divisions and Subdivisions: Quebec* (three volumes). Ottawa: Minister of Supply and Services, 1987; Canada. Statistics Canada, *Profiles—Census Tracts: Montreal* (two volumes). Ottawa: Minister of Supply and Services, 1988.

Albert and Shaw produce several maps in their book, but these are very small in scale. In consequence, I have had to put a little guesswork into the exact location of some of their borderlines. This has an impact upon the populations of the political divisions shown on my representation of their proposals.

I have assumed that the most logical position for the border between the territory added to New Brunswick and the new province of West Quebec is along the existing boundary between Kamouraska and Temiscouata counties. This seems to be consistent with their maps.

The western border of the territory to be awarded to Newfoundland is uneven, suggesting that it follows the course of a river. I have therefore placed it along the Romaine River, which flows from Labrador to the Gulf of St. Lawrence, east of Sept-Iles. —S.R.

Fig. 7   *Sources:* Kenneth McDonald, *Keeping Canada Together*. Toronto: Ramsay Business Systems, 1991; Canada. Statistics Canada, *Population and Dwelling Characteristics—Census Divisions and Subdivisions: Quebec* (three volumes). Ottawa: Minister of Supply and Services, 1987.

As with Albert and Shaw's plan, the proposed borders in *Keeping Canada Together* are illustrated in very small-scale maps. A verbal description is also given, but it is not precise. Accurate interpretations of population figures are therefore difficult. McDonald's plan seems to be largely modelled on Albert and Shaw's proposals in *Partition: The Price of Quebec's Independence.* I have therefore assumed that some of the borders in his plan are in the same location as those in the Albert-Shaw Plan. This is how I have interpreted the western borders of the territories assigned to New Brunswick and Newfoundland. The northern border of the republic of Quebec is more difficult to interpret. For the sake of convenience in calculating population figures, I have assumed this border to lie along the height of the land, which is also the old border between Quebec and Rupert's Land. —S.R.

Fig. 8   *Sources:* David Bercuson and Barry Cooper, *Deconfederation: Canada without Quebec.* Toronto: Key Porter, 1991, pp. 147- 157; Canada. Statistics Canada, *Population and Dwelling Characteristics—Census Divisions and Subdivisions: Quebec* (three volumes). Ottawa: Minister of Supply and Services, 1987; Canada. Statistics Canada, *Profiles—Census Tracts: Montreal* (two volumes). Ottawa: Minister of Supply and Services, 1988.

Bercuson and Cooper do not provide a map for their plan, and tend to be vague when describing the areas to be retained by Canada on the basis of self-determination. In mapping the extent of these areas, I have relied on three factors. In descending order of importance, these are: the descriptions of the areas (page 156 of *Deconfederation*); the injunction (also on page 156) that "the non-French have the right to secede from Quebec," which I interpret to mean that only non-francophone municipalities would be excised from Quebec when this is possible; and the overriding concern with military security. I have tried, on the basis of these criteria, to make their plan appear as reasonable and practical as possible, by my own standards. Nevertheless, the map remains largely interpretive and may not completely reflect the intentions of the authors. —S.R.

Fig. 9   *Sources:* David Varty, *Who Gets Ungava?* Vancouver: Varty and Company, 1991; Canada. Statistics Canada, *Population and Dwelling Characteristics—Census Divisions and Subdivisions: Quebec* (three volumes). Ottawa: Minister of Supply and Services, 1987.

The main ambiguity in David Varty's proposal lies in the extent of the territory he would be willing to cede to Quebec in return for compensation. He states only that the land in question lies in the extreme south of the Ungava region. It strikes me that the most reasonable interpretation of this description is the division of Ungava into two sections: 1. the provincial ridings of Abitibi-est and Abitibi-ouest (both located in the Rouyn/Val d'Or area in the extreme south of the territory transferred to Quebec in 1898, and both overwhelmingly francophone); 2. the riding of Ungava, which has a mixed population and which covers all the rest of the territorial cessions of 1898 and 1912. The first of the two sections would be offered to Quebec. I have based the population figures listed on the map on this interpretation. —S.R.

Fig. 10   *Source:* Quebec. Commission de la représentation électorale, *The Electoral Map of Quebec.* Quebec City: Directeur général des élections, 1980; Quebec. Directeur général des élections, *Rapport des résultats officiels du scrutin: référendum du 20 mai 1980.* Quebec City: Editeur officiel du Québec, 1980.

Fig. 11   *Sources:* Canada. Statistics Canada, *Population and Dwelling Characteristics—Census Divisions and Subdivisions: New Brunswick* (two volumes). Ottawa: Minister of Supply and Services, 1987; Canada. Statistics Canada, *Population and Dwelling Characteristics—Census Divisions and Subdivisions: Ontario* (three volumes). Ottawa: Minister of Supply and Services, 1987; Canada. Statistics Canada, *Population and Dwelling Characteristics—Census Divisions and Subdivisions: Quebec* (three volumes). Ottawa: Minister of Supply and Services, 1987; Canada. Statistics Canada, *Profiles—Census Tracts: Montreal* (two volumes). Ottawa: Minister of Supply and Services, 1988; Canada. Statistics Canada, *Profiles—Census Tracts: Ottawa-Hull* (two volumes). Ottawa: Minister of Supply and Services, 1988; Quebec. Directeur général des élections, *Rapport des Résultats officiels du scrutin de 25 septembre 1989.* Quebec City: Editeur officiel du Québec, 1989; Quebec. Directeur général des élections, *Dossiers socio-économiques.* St-Foy, Quebec: Directeur général des élections, August 1989.

Fig. 12   *Source:* Canada. Statistics Canada, *Population and Dwelling Characteristics—Census Divisions and Subdivisions: Quebec* (three volumes). Ottawa: Minister of Supply and Services, 1987.

Fig. 13   *Sources:* Canada. Statistics Canada, *Population and Dwelling Characteristics—Census Divisions and Subdivisions: Quebec* (three volumes). Ottawa: Minister of Supply and Services, 1987; Quebec. Directeur général des élections, *Rapport des Résultats officiels du scrutin de 25 septembre 1989.* Quebec City: Editeur officiel du Québec, 1989; Quebec. Directeur général des élections, Dossiers socio-économiques. St-Foy, Quebec: Directeur général des élections, August 1989.

Fig. 14   *Source:* Canada. Statistics Canada, *Population and Dwelling Char-acteristics—Census Divisions and Subdivisions: Quebec* (three vol-umes). Ottawa: Minister of Supply and Services, 1987.

Fig. 15   *Sources:* Canada. Statistics Canada, *Population and Dwelling Char-acteristics—Census Divisions and Subdivisions: Quebec* (three vol-umes). Ottawa: Minister of Supply and Services, 1987; Quebec. Directeur général des élections, *Rapport des Résultats officiels du scrutin de 25 septembre 1989.* Quebec City: Editeur officiel du Québec, 1989; Quebec. Directeur général des élections, *Dossiers socio-économiques.* St-Foy, Quebec: Directeur général des élections, August 1989.

Fig. 16   *Source:* Quebec. Directeur général des élections, *Dossiers socio-économiques.* St-Foy, Quebec: Directeur général des élections, Au-gust 1989.

Fig. 17   *Sources:* Canada. Statistics Canada, *Population and Dwelling Char-acteristics—Census Divisions and Subdivisions: Quebec* (three vol-umes). Ottawa: Minister of Supply and Services, 1987; Canada. Statistics Canada, *Profiles—Census Tracts: Montreal* (two vol-umes). Ottawa: Minister of Supply and Services, 1988; Quebec. Directeur général des élections, *Rapport des Résultats officiels du scrutin de 25 septembre 1989.* Quebec City: Editeur officiel du Québec, 1989; Quebec. Directeur général des élections, *Dossiers socio-économiques.* St-Foy, Quebec: Directeur général des élections, August 1989.

Fig. 18   *Sources:* Canada. Statistics Canada, *Population and Dwelling Char-acteristics—Census Divisions and Subdivisions: Quebec* (three vol-umes). Ottawa: Minister of Supply and Services, 1987; Canada. Statistics Canada, *Profiles—Census Tracts: Montreal* (two vol-umes). Ottawa: Minister of Supply and Services, 1988.

Fig. 19   *Sources:* Canada. Statistics Canada, *Population and Dwelling Char-acteristics—Census Divisions and Subdivisions: Quebec* (three vol-umes). Ottawa: Minister of Supply and Services, 1987; Quebec. Directeur général des élections, *Rapport des Résultats officiels du scrutin de 25 septembre 1989.* Quebec City: Editeur officiel du Québec, 1989; Quebec. Directeur général des élections, *Dossiers socio-économiques.* St-Foy, Quebec: Directeur général des élections, August 1989.

Fig. 20-   *Source:* United States and Panama. *Convention Regarding the Colón
22   Corridor and Certain Other Corridors through the Canal Zone.* 24 May, 1950.

Fig. 24   *Source:* Louis Malvoz, "Baerle-Duc et Baerle-Nassau: Trente-quartre Territoires pour Deux Communes," in *Crédit Communal de Belgique, Bulletin Trimestriel,* #155, January 1986.

Fig. 25   *Sources:* Canada. Statistics Canada, *Population and Dwelling Char-acteristics—Census Divisions and Subdivisions: Quebec* (three volumes). Ottawa: Minister of Supply and Services, 1987; Quebec. Commission de la représentation électorale. *A Fair Approach to Voting: Territorial Proportionality.* Quebec City: Directeur général des élections, 1984.

Fig. 26   *Source:* Map supplement to United States and Panama, *Panama Canal Treaty.* 7 September, 1977.

Fig. 27   *Sources:* Hydro-Québec, *Hydro-Québec Development Plan 1988-1990: Horizon 1997.* Montreal: 1988; Hydro-Québec, *Proposed Hydro-Québec Development Plan 1990-1992: Horizon 1999.* Montreal: 1990; Quebec, *James Bay and Northern Québec Agreement.* Quebec City: Editeur officiel du Québec, 1976.

Fig. 28   *Source:* Quebec. Commission de la représentation électorale du Québec. *La carte électorale du Québec.* Quebec City: Directeur général des élections, 1989.

Bibliography

Books/Scholarly Works

Albert, Lionel and Shaw, William. *Partition: The Price of Quebec's Independence*. Montreal: Thornhill, 1980.

Barlow, Maude and Campbell, Bruce. *Take Back the Nation*. Toronto: Key Porter, 1991.

Bercuson, David Jay and Cooper, Barry. *Deconfederation: Canada Without Quebec*. Toronto: Key Porter, 1991.

Berton, Pierre. *Klondike*. Toronto: McClelland and Stewart, 1972.

Black, Conrad. *Duplessis*. Toronto: McClelland and Stewart, 1977.

Bonifacic, Anton and Mihanovich, Clement, editors. *The Croatian Nation*. New York: Croatia Cultural Publishing Center, 1955.

Brossard, Jacques. *L'accession a la souveraineté et le cas du Québec*. Montreal: Les presses de l'université de Montréal, 1976.

_____. *Le territoire Québécois*. Montreal: Les presses de l'université de Montréal, 1970.

Brun, Henri, ed. *Le territoire du Québec*. Quebec City: Les presses de l'université Laval, 1974.

Cameron, Neil. "The Federalists of Quebec, the Separatists, and the Prospects of Partition." Speech delivered at the Airport Hilton, Dorval, Quebec: 21 February, 1991.

Charbonneau, Jean-Pierre and Paquette, Gilbert. *L'Option*. Montreal: Les éditions de l'Homme, 1978.

Domeniconi, Robert. *Le Canton du Jura: Statistiques Graphiques 1970 - 1975*. Delémont, Switzerland: Service d'Information de l'Assemblée constituante, 1978.

Donnelly, D.K. *Canamerican Union Now!* Toronto: Griffin House, 1978.

Dorion, H. *La Frontière Québec-Terre-Neuve*. Quebec City: Presses de la université Laval, 1963.

Drouin, Marie-Josée and Bruce-Biggs, Brian. *Canada Has a Future*. Toronto: McClelland and Stewart, 1978.

Eagleton, Clyde. "The Use of the Waters of International Rivers," in *Canadian Bar Review*. 1955. pp. 1018-1034.

Eterovich, Francis and Spalatin, Christopher. *Croatia: Land, People, Culture*. Toronto: University of Toronto Press, 1970.

Fidler, Richard, editor and translator. *Canada, Adieu? Quebec Debates its Future.* Lantzville, British Columbia and Halifax: Oolichan Books and The Institute for Public Policy, 1991.

Gazi, Stephen. *A History of Croatia.* New York: Philosophical Library, 1973.

Grady, Patrick. *A Survey of the Literature on the Costs and Benefits of Confederation.* Report Submitted to Strategic Policy and Planning Branch, Employment and Immigration Canada. Ottawa: 12 February, 1991.

Hand, Geoffrey, editor. *Report of the Irish Boundary Commission.* Shannon, Ireland, 1969.

Harbron, John. *Canada Without Quebec.* Don Mills, Ontario: Musson Book Company, 1977.

Jenkins, John. *Jura Separatism in Switzerland.* Oxford: Clarendon Press, 1986.

Lawford, H.J. "Treaties and Rights of Transit on the St. Lawrence," in *Canadian Bar Review,* 1961. pp. 577-602.

Lévesque, René. "For an Independent Quebec," in *Foreign Affairs.* July 1976. pp. 741-744.

_____. *An Option for Quebec.* Toronto: McClelland and Stewart, 1968.

Luthy, Herbert. *Une proposition pour le Jura.* Neuchatel, Switzerland: Editions de la Baconnière, 1972.

Malvoz, Louis. "Baerle-Duc et Baerle-Nassau: Trente-quatre Territoires pour Deux Communes" in *Crédit Communal de Belgique, Bulletin Trimestriel,* #155, January 1986.

McDonald, Kenneth. *Keeping Canada Together.* Toronto: Ramsey Business Systems, 1990.

McRae, Kenneth. *Conflict and Compromise in Multilingual Societies: Switzerland.* Waterloo, Ontario: Wilfrid Laurier University Press, 1983.

Nash, Knowlton. *Visions of Canada.* Toronto: McClelland and Stewart, 1991.

National Film Board of Canada. *Between Friends/Entre Amis.* Toronto: McClelland and Stewart, 1976.

Nicholson, Norman L. *The Boundaries of the Canadian Confederation.* Toronto: Macmillan of Canada, 1979.

Phillips, Arthur. *The Beachead Principle.* Toronto: Simon and Pierre, 1977.

Positive Action Committee. *Montreal: Present and Future.* Phase I Preliminary Report and Head Office Survey. Montreal: 20 June, 1979.

Resnick, Philip. *Toward a Canada-Quebec Union.* Montreal and Kingston: McGill-Queen's University Press, 1991.

Robertson, Ian Ross. "The Atlantic Provinces and the Territorial Question," in J.L. Granatstein and Kenneth McNaught, *English Canada Speaks Out,* Toronto: Doubleday, 1991.

Rudin, Ronald. *The Forgotten Quebecers: A History of English-Speaking Quebec, 1759-1980.* Quebec City: Institut québécois de recherche sur la culture, 1985.

Scowen, Reed. *A Different Vision: The English in Quebec in the 1990s.* Don Mills, Ontario: Maxwell Macmillan Canada, 1991.

Simeon, Richard and Janigan, Mary (editors). *Toolkits and Building Blocks: Constructing a New Canada.* Toronto: C.D. Howe Institute, 1991.

Thompson, John. "Unsettling Thoughts: The Security Implications of an

Usher, D. "The English Response to the Prospect of the Separation of Quebec," in *Canadian Public Policy*. Winter 1978. pp. 57-70.

Varty, David. *Who Gets Ungava?* Vancouver: Varty and Company, 1991.

Newspaper/Magazine Articles

Albert, Lionel. "Grappling with New Geography," in *The Citizen*. Ottawa: 4 April, 1991, p. A13.

_____. "Separatism a Territorial Matter," in *The Financial Post*. 29 April, 1991.

Arnett, James. "The Québécois Can't Take It All With Them," in *The Globe and Mail*. Toronto: 10 October, 1991. p. A21.

Arpin, Claude. "Option Canada Ripe for Big League," in *The Gazette*. Montreal: 29 April, 1991. p. A1.

Bisson, Bruno. "Les Cris entendent créer leur legislature." in *La Presse*. Montreal: 9 August, 1991. p. A2.

Block, Irwin. "Ryan Spurns Partition Idea as Negative Speculation," in *The Gazette*. Montreal: 19 March, 1991. p. A4.

Blohm, Robert. "Quebec Leads the Way in Foreign Borrowing," in *The Financial Post*. 8 March, 1991. p. 10.

Branswell, Jack. "Crees Wage David-Goliath Battle to Halt Hydro Dam," in *The Citizen*. Ottawa: 21 May, 1991. p. A4.

Brun, Henri. "Quebec Will Remain Intact If It Chooses to Separate," in *The Financial Post*. 17 February, 1992. p. S4.

Carleton, Evelyn and Carleton, Brian. "Include Us In," in *The Citizen*. Ottawa: 13 April, 1991. p. B7.

Cauchon, Paul. "L'inéluctable autodétermination des Inuit," in *Le Devoir*. Montreal: 22 July, 1991. p. 9.

Citizen, The. Editorial. "Merchants Back Idea of English Enclaves in Sovereign Quebec." Ottawa: 30 March, 1991. p. A5.

Creighton, Donald. "No More Concessions: If Quebec Does Go, Let It Not Be With Impunity," in *Maclean's*. 27 June, 1977. pp. 24-27.

Curran, Peggy. "Listen To Our Sovereignty Demands: Natives," in *The Gazette*. Montreal: 23 March, 1991. p. B4.

_____. "Disgruntled Outaouais Anglos Eyeing Ontario-Again," in *The Gazette*. Montreal: 3 March, 1991. p. B4.

Delisle, Norman. "Quebec Inuit Vote For Own Constitution," in *The Citizen*. Ottawa: 20 April, 1991. p. A8.

Dubé, Francine, "Hell No: Pontiac Group Wants No Part of Separate Quebec," in *The Citizen*. Ottawa: 30 March, 1991. p. A1.

Ferguson, Alan. "Croatian Territorial Concessions Rejected," in *The Star*. Toronto: 19 August, 1991. p. A14.

Globe and Mail, The. Editorial. "Quebec town wants to separate." Toronto: 24 January, 1981. p. A11.

Gratton, Michel. "Carving up Canada," in *The Sun*. Toronto: 7 April, 1991.

Hamilton, Graeme. "Separation Would Kill James Bay Treaty: Cree," in *The Gazette*. Montreal: 11 March, 1991. p. A4.

Maclean's. "Maclean's Q&A: Brian Mulroney." 6 January, 1992. pp. 68-71.

_____. "What If?" (special section on partition and the prospects of violence). 25 November, 1991. pp. 20-29.

Manchee, Rod. Letter to the editor, in *Saturday Night*. September 1991. p. 8.

Maser, Peter. "Divorce, If It Must Come, Could Be Nasty or Civilized—Poll Finds Potential For Both," in *The Gazette*. Montreal: 7 June, 1991. p. A8.

McIlroy, Anne. "Cree Set to Stop James Bay 2," in *The Gazette*. Montreal: 27 April, 1991. p. B4.

Montgomery, Sue. "'Get On With It,' Parizeau Tells Sovereignty Committee," in *The Citizen*. Ottawa: 3 August, 1991. p. A3.

Norris, Alexander. "Most Indians Would Choose Canada if Quebec Splits: First Nation Leader," in *The Gazette*. Montreal: 11 August, 1991. p. A5.

_____. "Cree to Debate Option of Seceding from Quebec," in *The Citizen*. Ottawa: 1 August, 1991. p. A5.

_____. "Inuit, Province Reach Accord on Talks for Self Government," in *The Gazette*. Montreal: 28 June, 1991. p. A4.

Picard, André. "Crees Vow to Seize Land if Quebec Separates," in *The Globe and Mail*. Toronto: 31 July, 1991. p. A1.

_____. "The Cree of Quebec: When the Bough Breaks," in *The Globe and Mail*. Toronto: 31 August, 1991. p. D2.

Poirer, Patricia. "Can't Carve Up Quebec Nation, PQ Leader Says," in *The Globe and Mail*. Toronto: 3 August, 1991. p. A3.

Sauvé, Peter. "We're Not Threatened, Say Ontario Francophones," in *The Suburban*. Montreal: 17 April, 1991. p. A25.

Setteler, Max Hugh. Letter to the editor, in *The Gazette*. Montreal: 26 March, 1991. p. B2.

Sudetic, Chuck "Croatia Endorses Independence Referendum," in *The Globe and Mail*. Toronto: 20 May, 1991. p. A1.

Varty, David. "A Separate Quebec Will Lose Northern Territories," in *The Financial Post*. 17 February, 1992. p. S4.

Watson, William. "Quebec Separatists Ignore Logic," in *The Financial Post*. 9 August, 1991. p. 9.

Official Documents

Berne. *Constitution du canton de Berne*. Berne, Switzerland: 1973.

Berne and Jura. *Accord-cadre regissant les accords provisoires fixant les conditions du transfert ou de l'utilisation des biens et les conditions d'utilisation de l'infrastructure actuellement commune*. Delémont and Berne, Switzerland: 1978.

Canada. Statistics Canada. *Canada Year Book, 1990*. Ottawa: Minister of Supply and Services, 1991.

_____. *Population and Dwelling Characteristics: Census Divisions and Subdivisions-Quebec* (three volumes). Ottawa: Minister of Supply and Services, 1987.

_____. *Profiles: Census Tracts-Montreal* (two volumes). Ottawa: Minister of Supply and Services, 1988.

_____. *Profiles: Census Tracts-Ottawa-Hull* (two volumes). Ottawa: Minister of Supply and Services, 1988.

Canada. Citizens Forum on Canada's Future. *Report to the People and Government of Canada*. Ottawa: Minister of Supply and Services, 1991.

Députation du Jura bernois et du Bienne romande. *Requête de la Députation du Jura bernoise et du Bienne romande aux Chambres Fédérales concernant la constitution du nouveau canton du Jura et plus particulièrement son article 138.* Tramelan and Reconvilier, Berne: 1977.

Hydro-Québec. *Hydro-Québec Development Plan 1988-1990: Horizon 1997.* Montreal: 1988.

Hydro-Québec. *Proposed Hydro-Québec Development Plan 1990-1992: Horizon 1999.* Montreal: 1990.

Jura. *Constitution de la république et canton du Jura.* Delémont, Switzerland: 1977.

Kanawetat et al. vs. La Commission hydro-électrique du Québec et la Societé de développement de la baie James. (Judgement of Mr. Justice Albert Malouf of the Quebec Superior Court, rendered 15 November, 1973; judgement of the Quebec Court of Appeals, rendered 22 November, 1973; judgement of the Supreme Court of Canada, rendered 8 January, 1974.)

Quebec. *James Bay and Northern Québec Agreement.* Quebec City: Editeur officiel du Québec, 1976.

_____. Commission de la représentation électorale. *A Fair Approach to Voting: Territorial Proportionality.* Quebec City: Directeur Général des Elections, 1984.

_____. Conseil executif. *Quebec-Canada: A New Deal.* Quebec City: Editeur officiel, 1979.

_____. Commission d'étude sur l'integrité du territoire du Québec. *Rapports.* Quebec City: Service de la reprographie.

Document 2.1: *La Frontière Québec-Ontario.* Rapport des commissaires. 1970.

Document 3.2: *La Frontière du Labrador.* Synthese. 1971.

Document 4.3: *Le Domaine indien.* Etudes juridiques. 1971.

Document 7.1: *Les Frontières dans le golfe du Saint-Laurent.* Rapport des commissaires. 1972.

_____. Directeur général des élections. *Rapport des Résultats officiels du scrutin de 25 septembre 1989.* Quebec City: Editeur officiel du Québec, 1989.

_____. *Dossiers socio-économiques.* St-Foy, Quebec: Directeur général des élections du Québec, August 1989.

_____. Secretariat des activités gouvernmentales en milieu amérindien et inuit. *Native Peoples of Québec.* Quebec City: Direction générale des publications gouvernmentales, 1984.

Societé d'aménagement de l'Outaouais. *Mémoire pour la Commission sur L'avenir Politique et Constitutionnel du Québec.* November 1990.

Ulster. *Ulster Year Book,* 1950. Belfast: His Majesty's Stationery Office, 1951.

United States and Panama. *Boundary Convention.* 2 September, 1914.

_____. *Convention Regarding the Colón Corridor and Certain Other Corridors Through the Canal Zone.* 24 May, 1950.

_____. *Highway Convention.* 14 September, 1950.

_____. *Panama Canal Treaty.* 7 September, 1977.

_____. *Treaty Concerning the Permanent Neutrality and Operation of the Panama Canal.* 7 September, 1977.

Index